Pursuing Teaching Excellence in Higher Education

Also available from Bloomsbury

Academics' International Teaching Journeys: Personal Narratives of Transitions in Higher Education, edited by Anesa Hosein, Namrata Rao, Chloe Shu-Hua Yeh and Ian M. Kinchin
Changing Higher Education for a Changing World, edited by Claire Callender, William Locke and Simon Marginson
Community-Based Transformational Learning: An Interdisciplinary Inquiry into Student Experiences and Challenges, edited by Christian Winterbottom, Jody S. Nicholson and F. Dan Richard
Cosmopolitan Perspectives on Academic Leadership in Higher Education, edited by Feng Su and Margaret Wood
Everyday Mobile Belonging: Theorising Higher Education Student Mobilities by Kirsty Finn and Mark Holton
Higher Education Research: The Developing Field by Malcolm Tight
Negotiating Learning and Identity in Higher Education: Access, Persistence and Retention, edited by Bongi Bangeni and Rochelle Kapp
Non-University Higher Education: Geographies of Place, Possibility and Inequality by Holly Henderson
Reflective Teaching in Higher Education by Paul Ashwin, David Boud, Susanna Calkins, Kelly Coate, Fiona Hallett, Greg Light, Kathy Luckett, Jan McArthur, Iain MacLaren, Monica McLean, Velda McCune, Katarina Mårtensson and Michelle Tooher
Syntheses of Higher Education Research: What We Know by Malcolm Tight
Transforming University Education: A Manifesto by Paul Ashwin
Understanding Experiences of First Generation University Students: Culturally Responsive and Sustaining Methodologies, edited by Amani Bell and Lorri J. Santamaría

Pursuing Teaching Excellence in Higher Education

Towards an Inclusive Perspective

Margaret Wood and Feng Su

BLOOMSBURY ACADEMIC
LONDON • NEW YORK • OXFORD • NEW DELHI • SYDNEY

BLOOMSBURY ACADEMIC
Bloomsbury Publishing Plc
50 Bedford Square, London, WC1B 3DP, UK
1385 Broadway, New York, NY 10018, USA
29 Earlsfort Terrace, Dublin 2, Ireland

BLOOMSBURY, BLOOMSBURY ACADEMIC and the Diana logo are trademarks of
Bloomsbury Publishing Plc

First published in Great Britain 2022
This paperback edition published in 2023

Copyright © Margaret Wood and Feng Su, 2022

Margaret Wood and Feng Su have asserted their right under the Copyright, Designs
and Patents Act, 1988, to be identified as Authors of this work.

For legal purposes the Acknowledgements on p. vi constitute an extension of
this copyright page.

Cover image © Martin Barraud / iStock

All rights reserved. No part of this publication may be reproduced or transmitted
in any form or by any means, electronic or mechanical, including photocopying,
recording, or any information storage or retrieval system, without prior
permission in writing from the publishers.

Bloomsbury Publishing Plc does not have any control over, or responsibility for, any
third-party websites referred to or in this book. All internet addresses given in this
book were correct at the time of going to press. The author and publisher regret
any inconvenience caused if addresses have changed or sites have ceased to
exist, but can accept no responsibility for any such changes.

A catalogue record for this book is available from the British Library.

Library of Congress Cataloging-in-Publication Data
Names: Wood, Margaret F., author. | Su, Feng, 1978-author.
Title: Pursuing teaching excellence in higher education: towards an
inclusive perspective / Margaret Wood and Feng Su.
Description: First Edition. | New York; London: Bloomsbury Academic, 2021. |
Includes bibliographical references and index.
Identifiers: LCCN 2021014302 (print) | LCCN 2021014303 (ebook) |
ISBN 9781350055285 (Hardback) | ISBN 9781350055292 PDF) |
ISBN 9781350055308 (ePub)
Subjects: LCSH: College teachers–Training of. | College
teachers–In-service training of. | Universities and colleges–Faculty.
Classification: LCC LB1738.W66 2021 (print) |
LCC LB1738 (ebook) | DDC 378.1/25–dc23
LC record available at https://lccn.loc.gov/2021014302
LC ebook record available at https://lccn.loc.gov/2021014303

ISBN: HB: 978-1-3500-5528-5
PB: 978-1-3502-1669-3
ePDF: 978-1-3500-5529-2
eBook: 978-1-3500-5530-8

Typeset by Deanta Global Publishing Services, Chennai, India

Contents

Acknowledgements	vi
List of Acronyms	vii
Preface	ix
1 Discourses of Teaching Excellence in Higher Education	1
2 Institutions' Perspectives on Teaching Excellence	19
3 Academics' Perspectives on Teaching Excellence	37
4 Students' Perspectives on Teaching Excellence	57
5 Employers' Perspectives on Teaching Excellence	77
6 Parents' Perspectives on Teaching Excellence	95
7 Towards an Inclusive Perspective on Teaching Excellence	113
Coda: Teaching Excellence in Challenging Times	131
Notes	151
References	154
Index	171

Acknowledgements

This book has developed out of our ongoing research in teaching quality in higher education. As academics, we are both concerned about the current dominant discourse of teaching excellence in higher education which tends to be narrowly defined and exclusive. In this book, we have attempted to develop an argument for an inclusive perspective by engaging multiple stakeholders in the debate on teaching excellence. We would not have completed this book without the support from a number of people such as colleagues and our students. Through conversations and exchange of ideas, they helped us develop our thinking and writing on the topic. Here we would like to thank the following colleagues specifically for their inputs.

We benefited greatly from conversations with Professor Jon Nixon, and we appreciate his generosity in terms of his time and intellectual support. We are grateful to the following colleagues who commented and provided feedback on draft chapters of the book: Dr Namrata Rao, Dr Chris Beaumont, Dr Richard Budd, Dr Phil Wood, Professor Dean Garratt and Andrew Pennington. We would also like to thank Dr J'annine Jobling who kindly commented on the final version of the book manuscript.

We would like to thank the anonymous reviewers for the critical but constructive comments they made on the original book proposal and the subsequent book manuscript. We would also like to thank the Bloomsbury team for their support and advice during the writing of this book, particularly Alison Baker, the Education Publisher; Maria Giovanna Brauzzi, Assistant Editor; and Evangeline Stanford, the Editorial Assistant. We would like to specially acknowledge the research participants who kindly shared with us their perspectives on teaching excellence in Chapters 3, 5 and 6.

Last, we would like to acknowledge that the book project has benefited from support from both of our institutions – York St John University and Liverpool Hope University. We also wish to record our thanks for support from the Centre for Education and Policy Analysis (CEPA) at Liverpool Hope University.

Acronyms

ACED	Ateneo Center for Educational Development
BAME	Black, Asian and Minority Ethnic
Brexit	A term used to refer to Britain leaving or 'exiting' from membership of the European Union
CHERI	Centre for Higher Education Research and Information
BIS	Department for Business, Innovation and Skills
DfE	Department for Education
EU	European Union
FE	Further Education
HE	Higher Education
HEA	Higher Education Academy
HEI	Higher Education Institution
HEFCE	Higher Education Funding Council for England
IT	Information Technology
JISC	Joint Information Systems Committee
MOOC	Massive Open Online Course
NPM	New Public Management
NSS	National Student Survey
OfS	Office for Students
PT	Personal Tutor

QAA	Quality Assurance Agency
REF	Research Excellence Framework
SoTL	Scholarship of Teaching and Learning
STEM	Science, Technology, Engineering, Mathematics
SU	Students' Union
TEF	The Teaching Excellence and Student Outcomes Framework
UCAS	Universities and Colleges Admissions Service
UDL	Universal Design for Learning
UK	United Kingdom
UKPSF	The UK Professional Standards Framework
USA	United States of America
VLE	Virtual Learning Environment
WURs	World University Rankings

Preface

Teaching excellence is a topic of international significance, having importance for higher education worldwide yet generally considered to be poorly defined and understood. In this book, we examine it through different lenses by engaging with a plurality of stakeholder perspectives. Opportunities to contribute to public debate about education as a shared public good are essential to the health and vitality of the public sphere, and the book develops an argument for the central importance of democratizing teaching excellence through engaging stakeholders in the development of understandings of this concept, what it means and how it should be enacted. The importance of enlisting different voices in discussions about teaching excellence in higher education to interrupt the current discourse and its ideological framing is the book's leitmotif.

'Stakeholder' is a term used in the business world and is also often employed these days in the lexicon of higher education. Such terminology reflects a particular discourse and positioning from business organizations which has spread through higher education and is rooted in a belief in competition and markets as the arbiter of quality and value. We use the term 'stakeholder' in this book to refer to the various constituencies of higher education, each with a particular 'stake' or interest in it. The discourse of consumerism, commercialization and managerialism in higher education is critiqued and contrasted with a view of higher education as a public good, what this means for teaching excellence and how it is to be recognized. The contribution of stakeholders to the development of understandings is conceptualized as a process of democratizing teaching excellence.

The performative culture of higher education, with the onus on measurement and quantification, is becoming deeply ingrained, such that it infiltrates and shapes thinking and drives practices. Teaching excellence as a fully formed concept must factor in the relationship between teaching and learning and the intellectual effort demanded of students. This is a far cry from the view of students as consumers, which misses the point of higher education as requiring intellectual effort and an active role for the student as a contributor to the learning process. The performativity and measurement culture focuses teaching excellence too much on teaching and quantifiable measures and underplays the role of learners, the processes of teaching and learning, and the qualitative relational aspects as a necessary part of teaching excellence.

What This Book Is About

This book explores the concept of teaching excellence and its framing in neoliberal ideological assumptions of performativity, new public management and competition, and argues for more critical, nuanced and sustainable understandings of how teaching excellence is understood and enacted.

Working from the premise that the current dispensation of higher education has been created by neoliberalism, this book argues that the introduction of the market has acted as a determining factor in the shaping of higher education teaching excellence. Teaching excellence is therefore seen as part of the creation of a higher education sector run on neoliberal lines, shaped by and responding to the market as the dominant factor in how higher education operates. This mechanism operates to make teaching excellence work in a market-driven way. With some commentators now suggesting that we are moving into a post-neoliberal era, it is timely to revisit and debate teaching excellence and also to think about who these debates should be with. How does teaching excellence fit into an emergent post-neoliberal order? It is an opportune moment to examine the discourse of teaching excellence and to wonder what teaching excellence might look like in the new dispensation.

This book does not claim to have the answers to these questions, but what it does is recognize that the 'old world' of teaching excellence, regulated by the principles of the market, must change in a new post-liberal world that may not have the same set of drivers. These market principles include self-centred individualism and a small state which desists from intervention but is also big on control and surveillance, together with competition and 'choice'. The Covid-19 global pandemic has highlighted and emphasized the shift to a new world in which we have come to accept that the state is important, and therefore 'what the role of higher education is' becomes a very important question. In a world reshaped, is it enough for higher education to be run along market lines, and what might this mean for teaching excellence?

We argue that greater emphasis should be given to the plurality of stakeholders' perspectives in higher education and that the dialogic space needs to become a multiple perspective debate on the matter of teaching excellence. We also argue for the debate to be reconceptualized in more democratic terms as a space for learning together across multiple stakeholder perspectives.

In our research for the book, in addition to drawing on relevant literature, we collected and analysed the primary and secondary data on how different stakeholders view teaching excellence in higher education. The chapters on institutions' and student' perspectives on teaching excellence draw on the secondary data publicly available. In the writing of the chapters on academics', employers' and parents' perspectives, we draw on the primary data collected through interviews with seventeen academics, seven careers advisers and eight parents. Additional survey data from sixteen parents was also included for the writing of the chapter on parents' perspectives. The details of each dataset are included at the end of each chapter as an endnote.

Book Structure

The first chapter examines the opaque yet ubiquitous and contested notion of excellence in higher education and lays the foundations for the central chapters of the book. This chapter explores understandings of the concept of teaching excellence in higher education and locates it in the wider political context of a competitive market-led education environment. It also considers some of the semantics and debates surrounding notions of 'excellence' as a popular and recurrent trope in higher education. It examines the discourse of teaching excellence in higher education as politically and ideologically charged rather than pedagogically driven.

In Chapters 2, 3, 4, 5 and 6, which form the central part of the book, we explore stakeholders' perspectives on teaching excellence. The stakeholder constituencies included are higher education institutions, academics, students, employers and parents. Drawing on empirical research and the literature, these chapters consider how teaching excellence is regarded from the standpoints of stakeholder constituencies. Parents are included among the stakeholder groups and, recognizing that this positioning is contested, we explain the rationale for their inclusion.

In the final chapter, we examine possibilities for the development of shared understandings from the above-mentioned stakeholders' perspectives and the institutional conditions that may make this possible. Stakeholder engagement in the construction of understandings of wider matters of the purposes of higher education, to which issues of teaching excellence are integral, is a challenging and vital task. It is especially necessary at a time when performativity and measurement hold sway and detract from a focus on the processes of teaching and learning. We argue that it is through engaging with higher education constituencies to examine teaching excellence from different angles and stances that more inclusive understandings can be built.

We use the term 'multi-stakeholders' perspectives' to recognize the plurality of stakeholders with different views who contribute to public debate about teaching excellence in higher education. This does not imply acceptance of the idea of 'the public's view' which, as we consider in more detail in Chapter 7 in our discussion of how stakeholder groups are defined and legitimized within the current system, we view with some caution. It may be appealing to suggest that these could be synthesized into one voice which captures these stakeholder publics' views. However, while believing that we can still legitimately conceive of a public realm, the plurality of the public sphere is central to this book and is conveyed in the term 'multi-stakeholders' perspectives'. This recognizes that within 'the public' there are heterogeneous broad groupings and interconnected constituencies with a diversity of positions existing in each. The idea of multi-stakeholders' perspectives embodies an implicit aspiration for a wider dialogue to construct shared understandings and a measure of consensus about teaching excellence and the purposes of higher education, to which issues of teaching excellence are allied.

At the end of each chapter we offer some review points for reflection, which have been prompted by ideas in the chapter and are intended to stimulate further thought and discussion. They are included by way of provocations, with the intention of inviting the reader to reflect and to continue the discussion. These are not intended as action points although they may inform potential actions.

The last part of the book was written during the global Covid-19 pandemic in 2020 and 2021. The crisis of the pandemic has provided us with an opportunity to review and renew our understandings of teaching excellence. The Coda explores some of the many changes and challenges to higher education related to the global Covid-19 pandemic and issues brought to the fore which demand a re-examination of institutions and their practices. The Coda considers the significance of these and their importance for future thinking and practice about teaching excellence.

1

Discourses of Teaching Excellence in Higher Education

In this chapter, understandings of the contested concept of teaching excellence in higher education are examined and located in the wider political context of a competitive market-led education environment, and some of the semantics and debates surrounding notions of 'excellence' as a popular and recurrent trope in higher education are considered. This chapter sets the scene for the wider project of this book, which is to examine what teaching excellence is considered to be from the perspectives of different stakeholder groups. It explores some of the implications of a discourse of excellence framed in a market-oriented higher education context and conceptualized in these sorts of terms. We question what this might mean for democracy, which in turn provokes further questions about the purposes of higher education and its value to society.

As we explain, it is timely to examine not only teaching excellence but also the role of higher education and the public good in ways that reconnect with and include the public as stakeholders of higher education, in examination of and reshaping the dominant discourse of teaching excellence. Lefebvre's theory of moments offers some purchase on possibilities evoked through the civic debate envisaged in the project at the core of this book, disrupting the neoliberal discourse of excellence and presenting an opportunity to reconsider and reappraise questions of purpose. The 'moment', as a 'recurring motif' (Middleton, 2014: 112) in Lefebvre's work, is defined as *'the attempt to achieve the total realization of a possibility*. Possibility offers itself; and it reveals itself' (Lefebvre, 2014: 518). The moment has 'a certain specific duration' (Lefebvre, 2014: 515); it 'reveals the possible' (Middleton, 2014: 181). The possibility to democratize excellence as part of a wider engaged civic discourse about the purposes of higher education may fill the current vacuum. We explore the possibilities to shape civic debate, by engaging the plurality of the public sphere, and Lefebvre's conception of the 'moment' as 'somehow revelatory of the totality of possibilities contained in daily existence' (Harvey, 1991: 429) has helped to inform this exploration. Regarding Lefebvre's concept of 'Moments', Shields (2004: 209) explains that it 'reappears throughout his work as a theory of presence and the foundation of a practice of emancipation. Experiences of revelation, *déjà-vu* sensations, but especially love and committed struggle, are examples of "Moments". By definition, "Moments" have no duration, but can be relived. Lefebvre argues that these cannot easily be reappropriated by consumer capitalism and commodified; they cannot be codified.'

Lefebvre's work has been drawn on and it is important to acknowledge that while employing Lefebvre's ideas, the extent of his work and influence is far broader and more extensive than represented here. Lefebvre is described by Shields (2004: 208) as a 'neo-Marxist and existentialist philosopher, a sociologist of urban and rural life and a theorist of the state, of international flows of capital and of social space'. Gottdiener (1993) described him as 'perhaps the greatest Marxian thinker since Marx, and certainly one of the greatest philosophers of our time'. His work 'Rhythmanalysis' which he wrote when he was in his late eighties (Middleton, 2014) provided 'a fitting end to his career' (Elden, 2004: 170). In this work, 'the abstract quantitative time, the time of watches and clocks' which has become 'the time of everydayness', is differentiated from the natural rhythms, 'day and night, the months and the seasons, and still more precisely biological rhythms' (Lefebvre and Regulier, 2004: 73). Rhythms 'interpenetrate one another' and music 'where the measure and the beat are linear in character, while motifs, melody and particularly harmony are cyclical' illustrates how rhythms 'may be said to embrace both cyclical and linear' (Lefebvre, 1991: 205–6). Lefebvre explained that 'What we *live* are rhythms – rhythms experienced subjectively. Which means that, here at least, "lived" and "conceived" are close: the laws of nature and the laws governing our bodies tend to overlap with each other – as perhaps too with the laws of social reality' (Lefebvre, 1991: 206). From our analysis of teaching excellence what appears to emerge are some of the ways in which rhythms of the 'conceived' dominate in a discourse framed, for example, by mechanisms of measurement and by commodification and quantification.

Rhythms provide a useful framing for our discussion of the hegemony of market logic and linearity and our thinking about the interaction with 'lived' rhythms.

The word 'discourses' in the title of this chapter refers to the language we use to describe teaching excellence, which is underpinned by certain ideologies, and sometimes even competing ones. This chapter explores some of the tensions in applying language associated with commerce and business to higher education and ideas about teaching excellence. The language influences the ways in which we think and speak about teaching excellence. However, discourses go beyond consideration of words and language; they 'constitute a way of acting in the social world as well as describing it' (Forrester and Garratt, 2016: 10). Within teaching excellence discourse, the language of the customer or purchaser, for example, constructs particular ways of being a student that may influence expectations of roles and behaviours fashioned by the logics of consumerism and market forces. We begin by examining how teaching excellence is conceptualized, shaped and fuelled by market logics.

Drivers and Conceptions of Teaching Excellence

Badges and trophies of excellence ostensibly inform consumer choice and, according to the policy rhetoric, choice is a driver and a spur to excellence. In this marketized world of higher education, the cost passes to the individual consumer in exchange for the benefits of future higher earnings which, in a deferred way, also acts as a tax on earnings at a future date, but one which is so far hence that it may not impinge on the thinking of students at the time. Arguably, too, the model is flawed if a large proportion of student debt is later written off, at a cost to the taxpayer. While a focus on productivity, employability and future earnings potential may present an apparently compelling rationale for higher education and its contribution to economic prosperity, trends have been towards a decline in graduate incomes and the underemployment of overqualified graduates. Ford (2016: 129) reported that 'Between 2007 and 2012, average starting salaries for UK graduates with bachelor's degrees fell in real terms by 11 per cent' while total outstanding student debt in the UK more than doubled. Participation in higher education is likely to mean high student debt incurred, with uncertainty regarding future availability of graduate jobs and graduate earnings. The potential student is faced with what we might term a 'double bind', the essence of which is captured in Blacker's (2013: 143) observation that 'The time has long passed when post-secondary education constitutes some kind of exceptional vehicle of social mobility, where four years of college places one on an upward path.' While a college degree may be considered necessary for 'the good life' and economic security, 'The education that was supposed to be the ticket *out* of a lifetime of economic difficulty is for more and more now a ticket *into* chronic economic difficulty. Yet it is still necessary as the alternative of not attending college promises even worse prospects for individuals' life chances' (Blacker, 2013: 128). The future 'upward path' and potential economic dividend for graduates appear to be uncertain.

Blacker (2013: 125) suggests that 'the cold-eyed context created by economic crisis' renders 'non-economic rationales' for education vulnerable. In some similar respects, conceptualizations of teaching excellence stemming from a 'non-economic rationale' are difficult in a pervasive market-driven discourse of higher education where the 'extrinsic "goods" that are easily quantifiable and therefore amenable to measurement' (Nixon, 2008: 60) hold sway. How might considerations of teaching excellence go beyond productivity, outcomes and cost to embrace intangible and vital questions of the value of higher education to society? This is a pressing concern given how instrumental views of higher education and teaching excellence have gained traction in a discourse dominated by metrics and outcome measures. Against the narrowness of this backdrop there is a need to rethink teaching excellence and to consider whose voices might be invited into this debate.

In the UK context, the Office for Students' overview of the Teaching Excellence and Student Outcomes Framework (TEF) (June 2019) says, 'The TEF measures important aspects that matter to students' and 'It sharpens the focus on teaching and outcomes that matter to students, by encouraging universities and colleges to deliver the best experience for their students and achieve higher ratings.' The TEF can be seen as one way of quality-assuring the value for money of their investment in higher education, quality-assuring the experience that students, as customers, have 'purchased'. The Office for Students website (Office for Students, n.d.) notes the role of the TEF as a tool to encourage excellence and inform student choice.

An environment of consumerism and customer satisfaction ratings does not sit easily alongside the idea of higher education as a challenging, though not necessarily always a 'satisfying', learning experience. If chasing student satisfaction ratings is the aim, then logically one option may be to minimize challenge and risk-taking and to 'play it safe'. By contrast, Healey (2011: 203) has argued that 'being prepared to take risks, and as a consequence at times failing, is integral to striving for excellence for both our students and ourselves'. Furthermore, New Public Management of higher education has encouraged universities to be defensive and inward-looking (Nixon, 2008: 22), which are arguably inimical to risk-taking, trying out new practices and innovative pedagogies. The issue of risk aversion and its implications for teaching excellence are returned to later.

The idea of excellence seems to be pervasive today in advertising and the marketing of goods and services, giving it the ring of a familiar and somewhat hackneyed refrain. It 'has become ubiquitous as a popular slogan' (Clegg, 2007: 91). So too in education, excellence is 'rapidly becoming the watchword of the University, and to understand the University as a contemporary institution requires some reflection on what the appeal to excellence may, or may not, mean', as Readings (1996: 21), writing in the North American context, suggested. Excellence can be understood in different ways, and with reference to teaching excellence, as Skelton (2005: 10) pointed out, 'Educational writing and policy documents often appear to assume that we all know what excellent teaching is, and terms like 'excellent', 'good' and 'competent' are often used interchangeably.' Lack of agreement about the idea of excellence was highlighted in Gunn and Fisk's (2013) review of the literature, 2007 to 2013, on university teaching excellence. They noted that 'How excellence is defined, operationalised, and measured in relation to teaching and learning still lacks a clear consensus' (p. 9). Similarly, prior to this, the CHERI report (Little et al., 2007: 4) had drawn attention to the need at a national level for further clarity about meanings attached to the term 'excellence'. However, opaqueness may be expedient for some purposes, and as Collini (2017: 43) observed, 'No determinant meaning can be ascribed to the claim that a university is "committed to excellence". Every institution presumably thinks that ideally it should be trying to do whatever it does as well as it can. Of course, it is "committed to excellence": what else could it be committed to?'

Making a similar kind of point, Readings (1996: 23) suggested that 'Today, all departments of the University can be urged to strive for excellence, since the general applicability of the notion is in direct relation to its emptiness.' Collini (2012: 109) has pointed to critiques of conceptions of excellence and the 'no standing still conception' of 'excellence', observing that 'the "excellent" must become "yet more excellent" on pain of being exposed as complacent or backward-looking or something equally scandalous'. In addition, 'Excellence, by definition, is a normative concept' (Elton, 1998: 4, cited in Little et al., 2007: 5), while Robson (2017: 114–15) has suggested that lack of clear consensus compounds the difficulties when challenging normative notions of excellence inherent in quality criteria and frameworks. Yet, despite the absence of clarity and agreement, the imperative to evidence excellence has become an all-important one for the higher education sector, and 'Those involved in teaching increasingly have to monitor performance and provide evidence of excellence to satisfy managers and external stakeholders' (Skelton, 2007: 1). The 'discursive migration' (Clegg, 2007: 92) of the concept of excellence from business to higher education and its implications for higher education discourse are considered by Clegg, who notes (p. 94) that 'Excellence, therefore, comes to us as a term with a particular genealogy and discursive location. It cannot be understood as a neutral descriptor, rather higher education has become colonized by a language not designed to debate the purposes and functions of higher education.'

Gunn and Fisk's (2013) reference to the measurement of excellence is a significant and vexed question, echoing the earlier CHERI report (Little et al., 2007: 3) that 'the current focus on teaching (and to a lesser extent learning) excellence is symptomatic of an ever-present contemporary desire to measure higher education performance by means of systematic criteria and standardised practices'. This point is echoed in Collini's (2017: 43) argument that a professed 'commitment to excellence' signals 'acceptance of the coercive fiction of competition' and 'implicitly, it also signals acceptance of the conventional forms of the measurement of achievement'. Discussing why excellence requires measurement using metrics, Saunders and Blanco Ramírez (2017) note how through the emphasis on measurement and comparison, the quantification of every educational act and outcome is normalized and that 'commitments to excellence require ubiquitous and commensurable measurements which work to reduce complex processes to simple quantifiable and comparable metrics'

(399–400). The market logic requires that data is collected and made accessible to students to demonstrate outcomes, facilitating comparison of universities and courses and informing their consumer choices.

'Teaching excellence' is in common parlance now in higher education and a manifestation of the influence of a particular ideology. Excellence can be understood as 'a technology of neoliberal ideology' (Saunders and Blanco Ramírez, 2017: 398) and 'the new currency of the higher education marketplace' (Nixon, 2008: 20). Attempting to come up with a unitary definition of neoliberalism would be ill-advised. There are different understandings and distinctions that are made as Olssen, Codd and O'Neill (2004) have noted, while recognizing, too, that there are some common features, including, for example, a belief in the operation of market forces and competition. Regarding the role of the state in neoliberalism, 'although its advocates subscribe in principle to a "reduced" state, it is a reduction of "bureaucracy" but not of "control"' (p. 138). Neoliberalism, described by Forrester and Garratt (2016: 197) as 'a modern regime infiltrating education policy at every conceivable level since the early 1970s', continues to influence how universities are managed (Nixon, 2008: 21). Mason (2016) suggests that 'Neoliberalism is the doctrine of uncontrolled markets: it says that the best route to prosperity is individuals pursuing their own self-interest, and the market is the only way to express that self-interest'. In the higher education sector, the impact of neoliberal imperatives has been felt globally (Gourlay and Stevenson, 2017). Collini (2012: 134) notes the political expediency of the business analogy: 'One of the supposed benefits of treating universities as though they were businesses is that their efficiency can then be measured and improved.' As a technology of economic exchange, markets operate through competition, and while this 'may in some cases be extended to work usefully in relation to other areas' (Olssen, 2010: 11), arguably there are some contexts where cooperation and sharing work better:

> Although it is essential in economic contexts to ensure norms of fair competition in order to avoid monopolies and the centralization of economic power, in many community contexts, including families, and frequently in work places, reciprocal social relations depend upon cooperative behaviour, and facilitation, rather than on competition. (Olssen, 2010: 11)

We may be becoming inured to the market analogy being applied to the university and to the importation of thinking and terminology from the commercial world into higher education, as Collini (2012) has observed.

Excellence and consumer choice are bedfellows in the market rhetoric, according to which 'Everyone can now buy into the excellence of their own choice – or so the argument runs' (Nixon, 2007: 15). Operating in a competitive, marketized system, 'universities now need to market themselves aggressively and compete to attract new groups of students. Teaching excellence is one way of staying ahead of the competition and securing a good position in exercises which rank institutions' (Skelton, 2005: 5). Ranson and Stewart (1994: 19) suggest that 'Consumerism provides an incomplete and ultimately inadequate language for the public domain. Its emphasis is upon the individual in receipt of a service, rather than on the citizen as an active participant in the polity.' The consumer is purchaser and receiver of services from the higher education 'provider', suggestive of education as a commodity which is delivered rather than enacted, an idea returned to later. As Ball (2013: 132) has argued, an impact of neoliberalism is that social relations and practices become transformed into 'calculabilities and exchanges, that is, into the market form – with the effect of commodifying educational practice and experience'. In the nature of this exchange, as between provider and customer, the notion of student agency becomes reductivist and impoverished as participation in higher education is seen more as a one-way transaction between paying customer and provider. This conception fails to do justice to the learner's role and contribution to the learning process: 'Customer implies paying for a service, but although students pay fees the essence of the contract is a two-way one in which they have to contribute much in terms of work and intellectual engagement if they are to succeed' (Clegg, 2007: 98). As noted in Gibbs' report (2012: 37), the use of the terms 'purchasers', 'customers' or 'consumers' in the market rhetoric fails to recognize the active participation of students in the teaching and learning processes: 'Students do not consume knowledge but construct it in a personal way in the context of learning environments that include teaching: they are co-producers collaborators.' With reference to the distinction drawn by Titus (Titus, 2008, cited in Saunders and Blanco Ramírez, 2017: 400), Saunders and Blanco Ramírez point to an important difference between helping to create educated students and creating satisfied customers:

> The former may have their prior ideas and political beliefs challenged, may be placed in uncomfortable learning situations that unearth embedded gendered and racialized assumptions, and may experience a sense of confusion and doubt concerning who they are and how they would like to

be in the world (Brookfield, 1995). The latter may expect their ideas not to be challenged but instead to be validated, no matter how problematic they might be. After all, students are paying for their education, and as the customer, they are always right. (Saunders and Blanco Ramírez, 2017: 400–1).

It is feasible that the consumer economy and the 'norms and expectations of our self-centred culture' (Roberts, 2015: 3) may have some bearing on this. The impulse society 'expects what it wants' and, explains Roberts, 'we are becoming a society that wants it *now*, regardless of the consequences' (p. 4). The idea that 'an economy reoriented to give us what we want, it turns out, isn't the best for delivering what we *need*' (p. 8) can be applied to a customer model in higher education. The notion of education framed so as to produce excellent customer satisfaction ratings may deliver what the customer wants and expects from education as a commodity. However, we should not lose sight of an important aspect of education which is that 'individuals often need to be told by someone who knows that a particular line of study is *worth* pursuing whether at the time they *want* to or not' (Collini, 2012: 185–6). Self-centred individualism undermines civic, social ways of being, Roberts contends, and engaging with, or even tolerating people or ideas that don't relate directly and immediately to us, becomes harder (Roberts, 2015: 3). However, this may be challenging and therefore perhaps not appreciated nor readily chosen. French (2017: 19) notes the heavy reliance of TEF on the National Student Survey (NSS) and that 'Worryingly, there is evidence suggesting that the NSS has certain potentially damaging in-built biases. For example, students report greater satisfaction when courses are less challenging; this has resulted in many lecturers becoming increasingly fearful of challenging students or taking them out of their comfort zone as it may result in low NSS scores.'

As discussed previously, risk aversion may be considered in some ways inimical to the pursuit of excellence for a number of reasons: for example, it may stifle creativity and innovation. Furthermore, the risk of unsatisfied customers may have implications for higher education study. The role and importance of higher education as something that seeks to 'satisfy' is arguably at odds with a pedagogy designed to develop active critical questioning and learning to respond to ambiguity, the latter being an important and pervasive feature of the world students are moving into. These may be unsettling and unsatisfying in failing to deliver neat solutions to complex problems, but a quest for easy answers is at odds with the experience of higher education study. Barnett has captured this idea well: 'The higher education experience should be a challenging and unsettling experience, opening the student's mind to a sense of ever-widening possibilities, in concept, supposition and approach to the world' (Barnett, 1992: 634).

Drawing on experience in the United States, Brookfield (1995: 252–3) suggested that student evaluation forms might be redesigned so that

> Instead of teachers being evaluated only on whether they pleased students (by means of forms that ask students whether or not they liked the teacher or the course), there would be items on end-of-course evaluations that would probe the extent to which students felt they had been stretched, challenged, questioned, and introduced to alternative perspectives.

This resonates with our argument about teaching excellence, higher learning and student satisfaction. A pedagogy of excellence might be considered to be more aligned to particular forms of 'student dissatisfaction', a term invoked by Collini (2012: 185) in a discussion of the detrimental influence of the student satisfaction scores when used as 'drivers of quality'.

In summary, the pursuit of teaching excellence appears ill-served by the model of consumerism with its inherent assumptions and expectations, where consumer satisfaction displaces the challenge and intellectual effort of higher learning.

Teaching Excellence, Measurement and the Purposes of Higher Education

The premise is that constructions of teaching excellence are bound up with market logics. Outcome measures reflect the influence of what Forrester and Garratt (2016) referred to as an 'economic turn' in education policy making and are beset with difficulties. These include a reliance on quantitative proxy indicators and a disregard for important aspects, termed 'intangible assets' of higher education by Robertson, Cleaver and Smart (2019), that are not quantifiable or measurable. Nixon (2007: 22) suggested that excellence is 'a process of growth, development and flourishing; it is not just an endpoint', and the importance of such processes and qualitative dimensions is missed if teaching excellence is boiled down to numbers. In Chapter 3, 'Academics' perspectives on teaching excellence', this line of thought continues as we explore teaching excellence in a conservatoire setting and the cultural value of the creative arts to society. Gibbs' report (2012) instances examples of universities adopting 'harder data-driven approaches' to review their performance against competitors and 'whatever the actual reliability or validity of NSS and other data, they are taken more seriously and given more weight than the kinds of observations previously made about the quality of programmes' (p. 22). The problems with 'using matrices to measure something as nebulous as teaching excellence' are also noted by French (2017: 16), and yet they persist.

Excellence becomes defined and represented narrowly by indicators that purport to provide some measure of it, and used to compare and rank provision. Consistent with neoliberal ideology, measurement is prioritized (Saunders and Blanco Ramírez 2017: 396) and 'previously non-marketized practices and social relations become commodified' (p. 399). There appears to be a lack of regard for the evidence in terms of valid indicators of excellence. Purpose is shaped by market reforms, and the contribution of higher education to the public good recedes into the background. Other institutions become competitors; the effort and the part played by students engaging in higher education is shaped by the customer orientation.

The concept of student-as-customer serves to reinforce a market relationship and the idea of exchange (Saunders and Blanco Ramírez, 2017). The 'redefinition of the student as a customer and the teacher as a service provider, and the goal of teaching being to create measurable indicators of excellence' (Saunders and Blanco Ramírez 2017: 405), have important implications. Wood (2017: 48) has noted what he refers to as the migration of individuals from being 'students' to 'customers' as 'HE has become increasingly market-based'. The concept of consumption orients the basis of relationships as economic transactions, and through free-market logic social relations become commodified (Saunders and Blanco Ramírez 2017: 399). Morley (2003) discusses the reconstruction of students as consumers in a chapter bearing this title, whereby 'Students are being reduced to their position in the market', and while they may have gained some 'leverage' as consumers, Morley suggests, 'more complex identities as scholars and social agents could have been lost' (Morley, 2003: 145). Nixon (2008: 11) has argued for the restoration of a way of talking about education, 'a public language of education and learning'. This is different from the ideologically imbued language of a market-led idea of higher education in which students are positioned in the customer role, the 'language of inputs and outputs, of clients and products, of delivery and measurement, of providers and users' (2008: 11). Nixon (2007: 31) has warned that vocabulary has been 'the most powerful weapon' of a 'dominant ideology of market-managerialism'.

Skelton (2005: 167) noted how 'Policies and discourses that have focused on teaching excellence have used it as a performative lever to drive up general standards.' It is perhaps unsurprising that in a commercialized environment, performative understandings of teaching excellence, as discussed by Skelton (2005), appear to reflect 'the potency of performativity' (p. 173). Ball (2013: 136) refers to 'the methods of *performativity*', in which 'productivity is everything'. Performativity is 'a key mechanism of neo-liberal government' and 'enacted through indicators and targets against which we are expected to position ourselves' (p. 137), but producing for many 'a loss of meaning in what we do and of what is important in what we do' (p. 138). Skelton (2005) suggests the need for 'a healthy debate about teaching excellence and a willingness to enter into dialogue with people who do not share our personal perspective' (p. 174). Saunders and Blanco Ramírez (2017) argue that post-secondary education's 'emancipatory potential' is diminished when excellence becomes an instrument for the enactment of neoliberal ideology.

In the competitive market of higher education, there is a range of 'providers' offering higher education. While the reference is to universities in this book, we recognize that there are different 'providers' of higher education qualifications and degrees, including Further Education Colleges. In a radio discussion about James Joyce and Ulysses, author Edna O'Brien (2020) spoke of Joyce contributing 'a new language and therefore a new way of thinking' and referred to language as 'the seed of thought'. Although the comment was made in a discussion on a different topic in a different context, this idea appears apposite. The language of teaching excellence now conjoined with that of market transactions between the higher education 'provider' and the 'consumer' influences how teaching excellence and matters of value and purpose are thought about. From a postmodernist perspective, what is 'real', as Legge (1995: 306) explains, is 'created through discourses emergent from power/knowledge relations', and 'Language is not a neutral vehicle for communicating independent "facts", but itself constitutes or produces the "real"'. The 'four Big Cs' are now the 'core business' of higher education: 'commercialization, commodification, competition and classification' (Nixon

2012: 9), and excellence has become a commodity (p. 11). Rowland (2008) has called for wider public debate about the purposes of higher education, and it appears timely not only to call for renewed debate about the purposes and the role that language plays in shaping thinking about this and framing the dominant discourse of teaching excellence, but also to consider who this debate should include.

In discussions of neoliberalism, the literature contrasts individual self-interest with common shared interests, social relations and the public good. Olssen argues that the idea of the common interest has wider importance for humanity when it comes to tackling some of the pressing global concerns of today such as climate change and its consequences, requiring a shift in thinking about what constitutes 'interests' from exclusively or primarily individuals to common concerns shared by all (Olssen, 2010: 21). We contend that trust is important as the foundation for the exercise of qualitative judgement to which Collini (2017) referred. Olssen, Codd and O'Neill (2004: 192–3) explain that trust is 'an attitude or disposition' influencing relationships and ways of acting towards others, and as 'a basic ingredient of cooperation', it can improve productivity and civic engagement (p. 193); however, its erosion is exacerbated by neoliberalism (Codd, 1999, cited in Olssen, Codd and O'Neill, 2004: 194). Examination of the premise that a competitive culture acts as a stimulus for the development of the quality of teaching raises questions about the assumptions on which it resides and about the wider implications for relationships and trust.

Quality and excellence may appear synonymous in many ways, but the literature suggests that these are not necessarily the same thing. Brink (2018) argues that quality is multi-dimensional, whereas excellence is one-dimensional. The many dimensions of quality, suggests Brink, 'should be valued rather than measured, and these must hang together harmoniously and reinforce each other for us to experience quality' (p. 189). By contrast, the one-dimensional concept of excellence is amenable to ranking and typically defined through competitive relationships with others (Brink, 2018: 189). But competitive cultures may fragment relationships and undermine collegiality, and whether the interests of developing teaching excellence are best served by competition and a culture of individualism is questionable (see Robson, 2017). In fact, market ideologies, competition and reductionist measures may erode the processes by which teaching excellence is best served when 'all of these ideological aspects of excellence work to foreclose the emancipatory potential of postsecondary education. That potential is based on cooperation, not competition; on creativity, not reduction; and on supportively challenging one another, not on satisfying a customer' (Saunders and Blanco Ramírez 2017: 401).

The idea of a lack of public trust in professional educators and educational provision was evident in Labour Prime Minister James Callaghan's Ruskin College speech in 1976, criticizing deficiencies of the curriculum as a preparation for work and to meet the needs of industry, and launching 'the great education debate' (Ward and Eden, 2009; Tomlinson, 2005). When public trust and confidence in educators is undermined, a justification for increased regulation and accountability measures may appear convincing, for as Nixon (2008: 21) suggested, the new public management of education was predicated on 'the assumption of a general breakdown of trust in the public and non-profit-making sectors and on the further assumption that public trust is best regained through systems of accountability that support competition across these sectors'. Understandings of teaching excellence and the dominance of metrics stem from the application of the logic of the market. Arguably, these are inadequate for the purpose: 'The measurement of teaching becomes the goal of the educative experience, and the dynamic and creative processes undergirding pedagogical performances are condensed to numerical expressions on a teaching evaluation' (Saunders and Blanco Ramírez 2017: 400).

Towards an Inclusive Understanding of Teaching Excellence

It is explained at the outset of the chapter that the argument for what we term an 'inclusive' and democratic approach to teaching excellence refers to the inclusion of understandings from the perspectives of higher education 'stakeholders'. Furthermore, 'inclusive' embraces considerations that go beyond productivity, outcomes and cost, and encompasses more fundamental questions which deal with less palpable matters of value, including the value of higher education to society. The current discourse of teaching excellence is narrowly framed, instrumental and linked to productivity and outcome measures. Against this narrowness we have argued for rethinking about teaching excellence which connects with ideas of the value of higher education in a democratic society.

In this chapter we have suggested that the current dominant instrumental market-led discourse is shaping thought about and understandings of teaching excellence, displacing conceptions of excellence as a process, a 'work in progress', and displacing debate about the value of higher education as a public good. Concerns about matters of 'value for money' appear to influence and shape ideas about teaching excellence, reducing the complexities of teaching and learning to proxy measures. This 'rationalistic' discourse has supplanted other ways of thinking about value: the value of higher education in a democratic society.

Recognition of the heterogeneity within stakeholder groups and the need to engage these diverse perspectives including minority and under-represented groups, is fundamental to an inclusive perspective on teaching excellence. The term 'excellence' has elitist connotations which may in itself appear oppositional to the idea of inclusive understandings. The construction of the concept of teaching excellence must embrace understandings and experiences of marginalized and under-represented groups in order to be inclusive. Monolithic and totalizing notions of stakeholder groups as being unified and homogenous, and Eurocentric assumptions about the experience of teaching quality that deny the situated and diverse nature of understandings and experiences, run contrary to an inclusive perspective.

The concept of inclusive learning and teaching is underpinned by values of equity and fairness (Hockings, 2010: 3). While a broader view of inclusive pedagogy which encompasses learners of all ages who come from different social classes and ethnic backgrounds is now more widely used in higher education in the UK, as Hockings (2010: 2) observed, this

> does not mean that the needs and rights of the individual are seen as having been addressed by virtue of their membership of any particular group or groups. Nor does it mean that individual identity is lost in the mix. It does mean, however, that we need to be mindful of the individual rights and needs of the 'diversity' of students in higher education today.

What teaching excellence looks like, for example, for minority ethnic students and students from under-represented groups, must be fundamental to an inclusive perspective, and strategies to connect with these voices must be found. As demonstrated by Cook-Sather's (2020) research study about a pedagogical partnership model in higher education, pedagogical approaches such as co-creation of learning and teaching can draw staff and student voices together in dialogue and help to develop more equitable practices.

In summary, the argument for what we term an 'inclusive' and democratic approach to teaching excellence has four strands. First, there is the intangible but vital question of the value of higher education in enriching people's lives and contributing to intellectual, creative and cultural innovation. Instrumental views of higher education and teaching excellence have gained traction, and against this backdrop, it is timely to rethink teaching excellence and reframe this thinking within a wider discussion of the role and value of higher education for society. As Robson (2017: 109) notes, across the world universities are impacted by new public management and neoliberalism as 'powerful political drivers of a quality culture'. The pressures to demonstrate 'excellence', construed primarily as 'instrumental goods' to the detriment of 'intrinsic goods' referred to previously, would arguably amount to a narrowly framed, instrumental pedagogical approach and an impoverished view of purposes and value. Relentless focus on outcome measures impoverishes richer conceptualizations that capture the complexities and importance of the processes of teaching and learning. Speaking of the 'intrinsic goods of learning' (Nixon, 2008: 60) acknowledges the contribution of relational aspects of pedagogic practice, and suggests a need for a more nuanced idea of teaching excellence which rests on the interconnectedness of the processes of teaching and learning. This is illustrated in Chapter 3 in the example of a conservatoire setting, which adds to the richness of our conceptualization of excellence. The illustration also raises awareness of the diversity and range of provision and learning environments across the higher education sector and the implications for the development of understandings and interpretations of teaching excellence in different contexts. Furthermore, an inclusive view of teaching excellence must reflect the diverse nature of higher education today through a commitment to finding ways to engage understandings situated in the experiences of marginalized and under-represented groups.

Second, we question how tables of rankings and ratings of teaching excellence support institutions to improve and develop teaching excellence. In an already stratified sector, it is feasible that, if tied to fee levels, low ratings may consign an institution to the bottom stratum indefinitely, thus sustaining and perpetuating divisions and hierarchies.

Third, drawing on the work of Blacker (2013), we have pointed to some of the effects when an economic rationale is applied to education, rendering a non-economic rationale vulnerable as, for example, matters of cost and value become conflated and confused. A market-driven model for higher education encourages institutions to chase customer satisfaction ratings, and yet, as we have argued with reference to the literature, 'unsatisfying' learning conceivably may be more aligned to teaching that prepares students for the ambiguities and uncertainties of the world they are moving into. It may not provide neat, 'off the peg' solutions and ready-assembled answers to perplexing questions. It may be difficult and challenging rather than satisfying learning, yet it remains an important and worthwhile component of higher education.

Questions of purpose are central to discussions of excellence in education, and this chapter has argued for the inclusion of stakeholder perspectives in building understandings. This argument for understandings from the perspectives of higher education 'stakeholders' to be included within wider public discourse about teaching excellence forms the fourth strand. The following words from Nixon (2007), which draw attention to education as a societal 'good' and act as a call for debate about democratic approaches to excellence, are germane to the argument in this chapter for public debate about teaching excellence and the role of higher education in society:

> If universities are central to the good society, then all those who value the good society must seek to regain that public trust and confidence. That can only be achieved through an open and honest debate as to how best to democratise excellence for the good of the university sector as a whole. (Nixon, 2007: 30)

Conclusion

Drawing on the literature, this chapter has explored some of the issues raised from an examination of contemporary conceptions of teaching excellence and some of the implications of recourse to a commercial vocabulary. In particular, the influence of this on thinking about teaching and learning, roles, responsibilities, behaviours and expectations have been noted. Through the thinking evoked in the use of such vocabulary, what is 'higher' about the learning in higher education is impoverished. Such vocabulary appears to sanction a consumer orientation positioning the student as purchaser of a commodity from a higher education provider, rather than a learner orientation.

Some of the key drivers and the potential impact of instrumental approaches have been examined and the construction of inclusive and democratic understandings of teaching excellence advocated. Higher education operates in a commercial environment and this 'leads inexorably to its *commodification*' (Nixon, 2012: 10). The market-led environment, in which higher education becomes a commodity, has shaped understandings of teaching excellence. This chapter has challenged these understandings and pointed to the need to engage public debate. Carr and Harnett (1996: 191) contrasted 'ideologically driven debate' with educational public debate, and the argument developed in this book is for the democratization of teaching excellence through the contribution of informed public discourse.

In the next five chapters of the book, perspectives on teaching excellence from members of the following key stakeholder groups are explored: institutions, academics, students, employers and parents.

Points for Discussion

- How does teaching excellence relate to the wider purposes of higher education?
- How might the language of teaching excellence influence thought and behaviours?
- How might different stakeholders view teaching excellence differently?
- What might be the potential drivers for the emergence of an alternative teaching excellence discourse?

2

Institutions' Perspectives on Teaching Excellence

In this chapter, we first consider international perspectives on teaching excellence in Australian and Russian contexts. The focus then turns to higher education in England in relation to institutions' articulations of teaching quality in their narrative submissions to the TEF.

International Perspectives on Teaching Excellence

As Skelton (2007: 7) noted, international perspectives play an important role in the critical investigation of teaching excellence and aid the development of understanding. We begin with a brief examination of experiences in the particularities of two different national contexts as examples, illustrating how policies for teaching excellence are enacted in each and the influence of global university rankings. Global rankings of universities and the worldwide quest for prestige are explored first, and teaching excellence in higher education in two contrasting cultural contexts is then considered. Our first example is Australia and, not wishing to limit our discussion to the Western world, Russia was also selected.

The context of global ranking is significant to the discussion of national policies. Blackmore (2016: 55) notes the dominant position retained by the United States in higher education international rankings; 'any international league table is populated heavily with US institutions', with the UK and Australia also described as 'relatively successful countries in terms of internationally prominent institutions'. Hazelkorn (2015: 1) referred to rankings as 'a manifestation of what has become known as the worldwide "battle for excellence"' and noted that 'there is a fascination with the standing and trajectory of the top 100, less than half a per cent of the world's institutions' (Hazelkorn, 2015: 2). Prestige may be conferred by being located in the upper echelons of such rankings and 'like the ranking of restaurants or hotels, no one wants to be at the bottom of the hygiene list' (Hazelkorn, 2015: 2). We might say that rankings can promote uniformity, exercising a 'hegemonic function' (Hazelkorn, 2015) in that 'they create a powerful set of ideas or values around which a particular model of higher education or concept of quality or excellence becomes the accepted norm' (Hazelkorn, 2015: 14). This idea connects with Biesta's (2011: 37) discussion of the rise of the 'Global University', and in the extract that follows this appears to be reflected in the author's repeated references to 'the same':

> The notion of the 'global university' refers to the fact that more and more universities in more and more countries all seem to be playing the same game and therefore increasingly are trying to become the same and to a large extent already have become the same. They all want to become 'excellent' and 'world class'; they all want to be research-led; they all want to get to the top of the league table; they are all chasing publication in a small number of journals included in a small number of global citation indexes.

Our attention now turns to some of the ways excellence plays out in the contrasting higher education contexts of Australia and Russia. In the Australian higher education context, Cooper (2019) argues that teaching excellence is unhelpful as a concept and is antithetical to good university education. In her view, the concept of teaching excellence has been used to distract attention away from discussions about funding and the conditions required to promote good teaching in universities. The construction of teaching excellence as an attribute of individual teachers has co-opted university teachers into supporting the illusion that teaching quality can be maintained, despite falling organizational support. Cooper suggests that universities have a responsibility to recognize the tensions between a view of excellence as an attribute of individual teachers and their 'individual performance' and a contrasting view of excellence which duly recognizes the teamwork which underpins good teaching, along with institutional support and reflexive self-criticality.

In the context of higher education in Russia, Tsvetkova and Lomer (2019) provide a critical analysis of the Russian academic excellence initiative 'Project 5-100', which aims 'at establishing a small group of leading Russian universities subsidized by the Russian government to bolster their global competitive advantages and to enter the top 100 world university rankings (WURs) by 2020' (Tsvetkova and Lomer, 2019: 128). The name 'Project 5-100' appears to signify the aspiration that at least five Russian universities would enter the top 100 in the world rankings and boost Russian competitiveness in the global education market. Twenty-one Russian universities were selected to participate in this initiative. The provision of state subsidies operated 'as a tool to rationalize the government's more active role in reshaping, modernising, transforming the 5-100 universities which as a result appear to lose their autonomy through the agreements signed to receive the state funding' (Tsvetkova and Lomer, 2019: 134). The authors describe the imposition of New Public Management (NPM): 'One of the ways to impose NPM on the 5-100 Universities is to stress the importance of enhancing "competitiveness" increasing "efficiency" of the state subsidies, improving the "performance" of the Universities, and consequently, tightening "financial control" and improving "quality assurance" of the Project' (p. 135).

Subsidies to the 5-100 could be discontinued in the case of under-performance. Research excellence dominated in the 5-100 universities, and Tsvetkova and Lomer's (2019: 141) study found that

> the Russian government adopts a narrow understanding of 'excellence' which privileges the research dimension over the teaching and learning activities, and emphasises it primarily as a tool to achieve Russia's aspirations for economic and social development rather than a target for enhancing and improving quality of research and teaching in the country's HEIs.

Tsvetkova and Lomer's study described a conception of excellence in higher education in terms of Project 5-100, its aspiration for at least five Russian universities to enter the top 100 WURs and how this appeared to focus attention on a small number of universities. Furthermore, NPM strategies were introduced in these settings, and state subsidies could be withdrawn in the case of under-performance. World rankings appeared to exert a particular influence, seen in measures to drive particular aspirations for international competitiveness and standing based on 'a narrow understanding of "excellence"' which, as Tsvetkova and Lomer (2019: 141) say, privileged research over teaching and learning.

Universities' Articulation of 'Teaching Quality' in England

In England, universities' articulation of 'teaching quality' is hugely affected by national policies on higher education such as the TEF. The TEF was introduced by the Government in England in 2016 for UK HE providers (TEF 1) with a single level award (Meets Expectations) when the minimum criteria for quality were met (O'Leary, Cui and French, 2019: 16). Participation in TEF 2 (2017) was on an 'opt in' basis, with assessment on the basis of metrics and a narrative submission (O'Leary, Cui and French, 2019: 16). Higher education providers in Scotland, Wales and Northern Ireland could choose to take part, even though higher education policy is a devolved matter (HEFCE, 2017). However, although some providers in Scotland and Wales participated, 'the TEF remains principally an English exercise' (O'Leary, Cui and French, 2019: 16).

The TEF was introduced to recognize and encourage excellent teaching in universities and colleges. The TEF uses a mix of quantitative metrics such as student satisfaction levels based on the National Student Survey (NSS) together with qualitative narratives submitted by universities to assess their own teaching quality. The qualitative narrative submission is up to fifteen pages in length. In the qualitative submission, universities are expected to cover three broad areas of teaching quality: learning environment, student outcomes and learning gain. Based on their overall scores, universities and other higher education providers are awarded a Gold, Silver or Bronze. The awards cover undergraduate teaching (HEFCE, 2017). By June 2019, 282 higher education institutions had participated in the TEF exercise – 76 of them were awarded Gold, 132 Silver, 60 Bronze and 14 Provisional. For those institutions that were awarded Provisional, it was because they had insufficient data to be fully assessed.

In this chapter, we analyse the 'teaching quality' section of the qualitative submissions from eighteen universities in England which have been awarded a Gold in the TEF.[1] In the process of data analysis, it was discovered that there was some apparent overlap between the categories, and the choice of heading under which to locate elements of the responses differed. Some institutions addressed the headings – student engagement, valuing teaching, rigour and stretch, and feedback – but in a different order; some addressed the headings through their own extended narrative form. Responses were therefore not uniform and this added to the complexity of the analysis. There were some apparent similarities across all submissions in our sample and, also, some features emerged which appeared to be more characteristic of the research-intensive (RI) sample of institutions, as we will discuss.

We recognize that the accounts are written for a specific purpose and acknowledge the importance of the rating awarded for institutions. While we are not suggesting any false claims nor questioning the integrity of the accounts, we are aware that pressures exist in a competitive environment where ratings may be used in marketing and advertising. We suggest that there is considerable self-interest at stake in the quest for high ratings and therefore an inherent incentive to present the data in the provider statements with this in mind. This is a consideration in reading the accounts.

There were two stages in our data analysis of the narratives from our sample of universities. At stage one of the data analysis, each of the authors examined the narratives separately and independently identified what emerged as the key ideas in each narrative under the given headings in the 'teaching quality' section. At stage two, the authors compared the preliminary individual analyses and agreed on the emergent themes. This was a form of investigator triangulation, which is where 'more than one person examines the same situation' (Wellington, 2000: 24).

Our analysis is of a sample of the whole population of provider submissions receiving gold awards. There were some common and recurrent themes in the submitted narratives. It was valuable to learn how each of the selected providers had evidenced teaching quality and how each presented this. It was perhaps not unexpected that there would be commonality in the examples selected, given that possible examples of evidence of teaching quality were set out for providers in the Teaching Excellence and Student Outcomes Framework Specification (DfE, 2017: 53). Furthermore, the assessed framework also included an explanation of each quality aspect (DfE, 2017: 24). The Teaching Quality aspect included 'The extent to which a provider recognises, encourages and rewards excellent teaching' (p. 24), and our aim was to understand these institutions' perceptions of teaching excellence through the choice and presentation of evidence for teaching quality in their settings.

There were four themes in the assessment criteria for 'Teaching Quality' narrative submissions in the Department for Education Teaching Excellence and Student Outcomes Framework Specification (2017): Student Engagement, Valuing Teaching, Rigour and Stretch, and Assessment and Feedback.

Student Engagement

In TEF, 'student engagement' is assessed through the extent to which 'Teaching provides effective stimulation, challenge and contact time that encourages students to engage and actively commit to their studies' (DfE, 2017: 25). The idea of 'engagement' is seen in the extracts below as being 'at the heart of' and 'pivotal' to provision. The term 'engagement' is frequently used, yet defining it is 'a contentious issue in HE' (Bovill, 2020: 25). Harper and Quaye suggest that 'student engagement is simply characterized as participation in educationally effective practices, both inside and outside the classroom, which leads to a range of measurable outcomes' and that finding ways to increase the engagement of various student populations, especially those for whom engagement is known to be problematic, is worthwhile (Harper and Quaye, 2009: 2–3). In the narratives, ideas about engagement, student voice and partnership with students appear to be linked together. In evaluations of teaching, students' views are often gathered via questionnaires, for example, but these can fail to capture the diverse nature of the student population as Okupe and Medland (2019: 262) have pointed out. Also, questionnaires can be blunt instruments for understanding the uniqueness of students' backgrounds that influence students' lives and experiences of teaching practice (Okupe and Medland, 2019: 262). Pointing to the need for pluralization of the concept of student voice, Okupe and Medland consider the appropriateness of the instruments used to capture these voices to inform the development of teaching practice, something of central importance and relevance for the development of teaching excellence informed by multiple student perspectives and experiences.

Sixteen universities in the sample articulated their initiatives for student engagement in relation to student voice and student partnership. Many universities have claimed that student engagement is part of their institution's strategies.

> Student engagement lies at the heart of our teaching quality and enhancement strategies. It can be seen and evidenced at every level of our governance structure, our feedback mechanisms and through our extensive methods

deployed to support students' learning. Our sustained excellent NSS performance highlights the effectiveness of this approach. (T9 university)

Active student engagement in education is pivotal to our provision and the student voice is at the heart of our strategy. We have, therefore, designed systems that ensure students have a strong voice across all aspects of our education provision. (R1 university)

Almost all universities have claimed that they have established a formal student representative structure to ensure that student voices are represented across their operations at different levels. At a strategic level, there are examples where students are represented on relevant institutional committees, such as the board of governors, academic board and learning and teaching committees, as well as on programme validation and review panels. National Student Survey (NSS) results are often used to indicate validation of the effectiveness of such approaches.

The student voice is embedded into our validation processes through their membership of curriculum delivery approval panels. (T5 university)

A recurring theme in our analysis of the institutions' narrative submissions is universities' embrace of the 'students as partner' concept in their articulation of student engagement. This encompasses many aspects of teaching and learning. There is also an emphasis on the universities' partnerships with students' unions. In their submissions, three universities in our sample included supporting statements from their student unions.

Partnership with our students is critical. The student voice is powerful and has led to direct improvements in teaching and learning. (T6 university)

These three universities also highlighted student engagement with their student-led staff awards in their submissions.

The Students' Union (SU) coordinates Student-Led Staff Awards, and the exceptional contributions of those staff who excel in teaching are celebrated annually at our degree ceremonies. From the many hundreds of nominations typically received, the SU thematically analyse outcomes and disseminate them at the University's Learning & Teaching Conference. The award winners also contribute their work to the professional development programme for staff. In these ways, students' views on the teaching they most value are embedded back into our practices. (T5 university)

In some universities, there are even dedicated personnel to look after student engagement and student voice.

> The University's commitment to student engagement is further evidenced in the appointment of a Student Engagement Facilitator (SEF). The SEF works with staff and students to improve the student learning experience and enhance the dialogue and engagement between staff and students. (T1 university)

> The University has in place a comprehensive student representative structure. The Student Voice team ensures that the student representative system works effectively and consistently across the University. (T2 university)

In addition to the NSS, students' voices are also captured and addressed by some universities through course evaluations, ad hoc surveys and focus groups. One university (R7) explicitly stated that student course evaluation results play a prominent part in the staff personal development and performance review process and have a significant impact on promotion decisions. In the USA, there are similar practices in academic tenure. Some might argue that this practice leads to academics adopting popular approaches rather than evidence-informed approaches for effective learning. At one university (T6), students were also trained to evaluate teaching.

For some of the research-intensive universities, the importance of small group teaching is highlighted in their narrative submissions as a way of engaging students in learning.

> Small group teaching (usually one member of academic staff meeting weekly with two or three students) is aimed at developing a student's capacity to think and write in depth about a subject area, to learn to operate with confidence within its methodologies and to foster precision of academic argument. It enables teaching to be tailored to the academic needs of the individual student. Small group teaching is demanding both for students and tutors, representing an intellectually challenging conversation between teacher and student, and between students, providing valuable opportunities for peer to peer learning. (R8 university)

> We routinely use small-group teaching to facilitate engagement (generating enthusiasm through up-to-date thinking and debate), interaction (immediate feedback), reflexivity (establishing an active learning environment for both

students and staff) and flexibility (iterative and dynamic learning). (R7 university)

At R2 university, small group teaching means that a small number of students (typically two or three) meet with a subject-specialist teacher for an in-depth discussion of a particular topic. Face-to-face contact hours are also used by one university (R5) as a way of engaging students in learning and teaching. At this university, students can expect to be in timetabled sessions for between twenty and twenty-five hours per week. Some might question, though, whether these face-to-face contact hours necessarily mean that students engage with the intended activities within the session.

Valuing Teaching

In TEF, 'valuing teaching' is assessed through the extent to which 'Institutional culture facilitates, recognises and rewards excellent teaching' (DfE, 2017: 25).

Unsurprisingly perhaps, most universities in this study have explicitly claimed that they value teaching, and typically evidence is cited from human resources processes for promotion exercises, available learning and teaching awards, internal learning and teaching funding, and ongoing professional development. In their accounts, universities also make explicit the links that exist between teaching and research. Commitment to both teaching and research is also apparent in the evidence for 'rigour and stretch'.

> Valuing teaching is embedded in our HR and CPD practices and is grounded in our promotion of the concept of the authentic academic, supported through the professional development of colleagues. We ask 'What gives you the right to teach our students?' and expect staff to have teaching, research and professional credibility. (T6 university)

> The University values high-quality teaching: evidence of 'effective contributions to undergraduate or postgraduate teaching' is a requirement for promotion to the senior academic positions of Professor or Reader, while promotion to the position of University Senior Lecturer requires evidence of 'sustained excellence in teaching'. (R2 university)

> The promotion criteria and annual performance review require academic staff to demonstrate a commitment to both teaching and research. (T7 university)

Such statements may prompt a number of critical questions, such as, for example, how providers define and judge 'effectiveness', 'commitment' and 'sustainability'.

In promotion exercises, some universities have emphasized equal career progression for both teaching- and research-focused academics.

> We recognise and reward teaching excellence equally with research in the promotions system. This includes a promotion route to professor 'for academic colleagues on teaching-only contracts who have made an exceptional contribution to teaching at the highest level of excellence'. We make no distinction in academic title between those who are on Research and Teaching, and Teaching-only contracts. (R9 university)

> We recognise talented academics who dedicate their careers to teaching excellence through the 'teaching-focused career-pathway'. Teaching-focused staff have the same career-progression opportunities as those on the research-focussed pathways, including promotion to Reader and Professor, and the opportunity to apply for study leave. (R1 university)

To highlight the importance of teaching and student education, universities in the UK have increasingly created senior posts in these areas.

> Our commitment to student education is advocated and led at the most senior level of the University by a Deputy Vice-Chancellor (Student Education). Each faculty has a Pro-Dean for Student Education, who reports to the Dean and Deputy Vice-Chancellor. (R6 university)

Different learning and teaching awards are also used by universities to demonstrate their recognition of outstanding teaching. These internal awards are largely divided into two categories – one is coordinated by the university's centre of learning and teaching, and another is often student-led and coordinated by universities' student unions. Award categories include the vice-chancellor's teaching award, outstanding student support, outstanding innovation in teaching, best employer engagement initiative and most inspirational lecturer. Six research-intensive universities also provide internal funding to support learning and teaching-related innovations or interventions.

> We operate three institutional schemes for excellence in teaching; two award outstanding current practice, as identified by our students, and one provides project funding for innovation and enhancement in scholarship. (R3 university)

Universities have also offered postgraduate certificate-level courses for their own staff to develop their teaching capacities. These courses are often aligned with the UK Professional Standards Framework (UKPSF) and accredited by Advance HE (formerly the Higher Education Academy (HEA)). These courses normally lead to HEA fellowship recognition such as Fellows and Senior Fellows. Both research-intensive and teaching-intensive universities use the proportion of staff holding a teaching qualification as an indicator of teaching competence and expertise. Peer review of teaching and an annual learning and teaching day are also adopted by universities to provide ongoing professional development opportunities.

Rigour and Stretch

In TEF, 'rigour and stretch' is defined through the extent to which 'Course design, development, standards and assessment are effective in stretching students to develop independence, knowledge, understanding and skills that reflect their full potential' (DfE, 2017: 25).

On academic rigour and stretch, universities often emphasize either their research-led or research-informed curriculum and teaching. For research-intensive universities, 'cutting-edge research' and teaching by 'experts' are often referred to.

> Our university education is designed to challenge and stretch all students. Courses and modules are based on cutting-edge research. (R1 university)

R8 university described, 'World-leading researchers as teachers in terms of passion for their subject, conviction about its importance for their students' intellectual growth, and the enthusiasm that is evident to their students' (R8 university).

For some of the research-intensive universities, in relation to intellectual stretch, the availability of cross-university common modules are often referred to.

> A cross-university initiative encourages all first year students to study up to 20 credits outside their main discipline drawn from our comprehensive catalogue of modules. (R1 university)

Based on NSS narrative results, some students have found it challenging to study at these research-intensive universities. These (research-intensive) universities have shown their awareness of this and have stressed the need for a balance between academic rigour and stretch and student well-being.

> The University is acutely aware of the need to find an appropriate balance between rigour and stretch on the one hand and student work-life balance and good mental health on the other. (R5 university)

> Following a review in 2015–16, precipitated by concerns expressed by some students about workload, courses are required to be clear about their expectations for the number of hours of teaching and independent study a student should do each week. The University designates a maximum student workload of 48 hours per week in term-time. (R2 university)

For teaching-intensive universities, strong industry links are often highlighted. Links with professional statutory regulatory bodies (PSRBs) are also cited as exerting rigorous external scrutiny and standards.

> The University is committed to an industry-led curriculum, designed in concert with employers, alumni and industry experts. The University has introduced industry advisory panels for each academic department to add value to the curriculum and the student experience. (T2 university)

> Externality is a key feature, not only of programme approval but also of programme design, with funding for external consultancy made available to all course development teams. (T5 university)

> Our unique curricular design and partnership with employers reinforces our real-world ethos. (T9 university)

External examiner scrutiny and Higher Education Reviews are also cited as evidence of rigour.

> All of our programmes are academically rigorous. This is evidenced explicitly by our 250 external examiners who unanimously endorsed our standards and successful 2016 Higher Education Review, which endorsed the effectiveness of our quality processes in assuring standards. (T9 university)

Formal exams are used by some research-intensive universities to maintain academic rigour and stretch.

> The University believes that summative written examinations, grouped together, provide a method of holistic assessment which allows students to

demonstrate the range and depth of knowledge and skills they have acquired and to link together learning from between different elements of their degree course. (R8 university)

While it is important to demonstrate that assessment methods are effective in that students are appropriately challenged and stretched, the need for balance and avoidance of assessment overload is an important concern, too.

The NSS results are used by many universities as evidence of the rigour and stretch of their degree programmes. Student responses to the following two NSS statements, concerned with 'intellectual stimulation' and 'academic challenge', are often referred to: 'The course is intellectually stimulating' and 'My course has challenged me to achieve my best work.'

A small minority of universities have used the proportion of first-class and upper-second-class degrees awarded as an indicator of student attainment.

> The proportion of 1sts and 2:1s awarded has increased from 78% in 2007–08, to 91% in 2016–17, with the proportion of 1sts rising from 18% to 31% over the same period. (R3 university)

While this is evidence of outcomes, this could arguably be achieved by a number of possible different means and influenced by a range of factors, including improvements in teaching and learning. The issue of grade inflation is a live issue in the sector and could potentially be another explanation for improved student attainment outcomes. In order to address any potential controversy in using the proportion of first-class and upper-second-class degrees as an indicator of high levels of attainment while maintaining the academic rigour and value of their degrees, one university stated:

> We monitor our proportion of 1st and 2:1 degrees, which is amongst the highest in the sector at 84%. In addition to careful triangulation with external examiners' reports, since 2015, Senate has commissioned an annual longitudinal statistical analysis of awards data. These analyses indicate no evidence for institutional or programme grade inflation. (R4 university)

Feedback

In TEF, 'feedback' is viewed through the extent to which 'Assessment and feedback are used effectively in supporting students' development, progression and attainment' (DfE, 2017: 25).

Assessment and feedback, crucial to student learning, have traditionally been challenging for universities in terms of student satisfaction. Many universities have attempted to address this through achieving a speedier assignment feedback turnaround time, the use of a variety of methods of summative and formative assessment, and the use of standardized approaches to ensure consistency in feedback and the use of technologies in the process of assignment feedback.

> The maximum time periods for tutors to mark, grade and provide student feedback on submitted coursework are currently 3 weeks for first and second year undergraduate students and 2 weeks for final year undergraduate and postgraduate students. (T3 university)

> Feedback on assessment has also been improved by the introduction of electronic management of coursework. This enables individualised feedback to be given speedily and conveniently to students. (R7 university)

Some universities have aimed to develop students' assessment literacy, a term which refers to students' understanding of the purposes and practices of assessment and feedback, and appreciation of their relationship to learning.

> We pay particular attention to developing students' assessment literacy to ensure they understand the purpose and forms of assessment, how judgements are reached and how grades and feedback align with intended learning outcomes. (T5 university)

In some universities' accounts, the availability of personalized support for students on assessment feedback was noted; this was usually through small group tutorials or discussions with personal tutors. Arguably important too are approaches to improving student engagement with feedback which may help to maximize its usefulness in supporting progress and 'feed-forward'. This can be understood as the 'forward-pointing aspects of feedback' (Race and Pickford, 2007: 116) to inform and support future learning. The timeliness of feedback is important (see, for example, Race and Pickford, 2007) in improving student engagement with feedback.

Implications for Practice

Common ideas apparent in many of the narratives such as 'student as partner' and 'student voice' and 'engagement' suggest that students tend to be positioned by the institutions as central to the concept of teaching excellence and located 'at the heart of their services' (Beech, 2017: 55). In our analysis, the institutions' narratives appeared to signal this prime focus on the student first and foremost while the structures, resources, processes and practices described conveyed a sense that their purpose was enabling and supporting students and their learning. Beech's study of provider statements from a sample of institutions having had their awards changed during the TEF process recommended that higher education institutions should show that students matter (Beech, 2017: 57), a theme we found inherent in our sample of narrative submissions. We have argued implicitly in our writing for the importance and centrality of intangible aspects of the pedagogical relationships between teacher and learner (Wood and Su, 2017: 462). Nixon (2008: 106) spoke of 'encouragement', 'helping' and 'reaching out' in teaching: 'Teaching is about encouraging people to learn; and encouraging people to learn is about helping them find reasons for taking their own learning seriously; and helping them do that involves reaching out to them beyond our existing horizons.' Inspired by these words and the findings of our own research study, we suggested (Wood and Su, 2017: 462) that 'reaching out', inspiring with confidence and developing critical capable learners may not sit easily within the current policy discourse. Our contention is that an inclusive perspective on academic practice may help to restore these things to a position of primacy in discussions of 'teaching excellence'. The inclusive perspective here also refers to inclusion of intangible aspects of academic practice, such as encouragement and inspiring learners with confidence.

The current higher education policy climate appears to be at some distance from this conceptualization. O'Leary, Cui and French (2019: 82) suggest that 'The TEF's processes, with their increasing emphasis on employability and graduate salaries, reflect an adherence to a quintessentially competitive market model of HE that actually has little to do with teaching excellence.'

In terms of the development of academic practice, it would be useful for institutions to consider what the market model of higher education and putting students and 'the undergraduate experience at the heart of the system' (Department for Business, Innovation & Skills, 2011: 4) means to them. Universities might reflect on how they can show that students matter as 'contributors' in a way that is not construed solely as financial contributors investing in higher education but as active contributors to the process of learning and intellectual work. In the narratives, how different student populations are engaged, how student 'partners' sits coherently alongside a dominant policy discourse of the student-consumer and what partnership is understood to mean appeared underdeveloped. Such a lack of clarity appears to be a feature of some of the literature in the field, too, as Seale et al. (2015: 534) noted, and while a growing emphasis is placed on promoting collaborative partnerships between staff and students across the student voice and engagement literature, conceptualization of voice and participation and theorization of partnership can be underdeveloped (p. 536). Seale et al. (2015) pointed to some apparent lack of critical awareness among policymakers of possible tensions between students positioned both as consumers and as partners, and the authors highlighted 'the need for a critical re-examination of how we conceptualise students as "partners" and the presumptions we make regarding the nature of partnerships between academics/institutions and students' (p.550).

Institutions' articulations of teaching excellence often appear to have a significant impact on academic practice. For instance, while some of the universities' contextual narratives emphasize the existence of equal opportunities for career progression and academic promotion for teaching and research, the existence of separate 'teaching-focused' and 'research-focused' career-pathways and the existence of the Research Excellence Framework (REF) and TEF sets teaching and research apart from each other. It is interesting, for example, that 'impact' in the REF 'does not include intellectual influence on other scholars and researchers or influence on the content of teaching' (Nixon, 2012: 10). Blackmore (2016: 131) has noted that 'one of the most hotly contested questions over the last twenty years has been whether and how research informs teaching, the so-called research-teaching nexus,' and he has discussed some of the beliefs and claims about the relationship between research and teaching:

> Claims have often been made that research funding for universities should be preserved, on the grounds that there is a teaching benefit. This may be driven by a sincere belief that this is so. Repeatedly, when surveyed, faculty declare that the presence of research activity is a benefit for education. However, it is also a convenient belief in that it protects a highly valued activity, research. (Blackmore, 2016: 132)

Blackmore also observed that 'even within the most favoured research intensive institutions', much of the teaching may be undertaken by teaching-only contracted colleagues and by graduate teaching assistants (Blackmore, 2016:

132). Ingold (2018: 72) has explained that 'there cannot be research without teaching', seeing both as 'practices of education, and both are inextricably linked'. In the findings from their research into the impact and implications of the TEF on staff working in higher education provision in the UK, O'Leary, Cui and French (2019: 6–7) pointed to the importance of recognizing the synergies between TEF and REF:

> TEF and REF are currently presented to staff as competing agendas and interests in many organisations. Findings from this study suggest that institutions have started strategically positioning their staff and resources to ensure desirable outcomes are achieved against each of these assessments. In some institutions, teaching is viewed and treated very separately from research, and consequently the two are often separated out into different job roles and contracts. The sector, institutions and policy makers need to be more mindful of the interplay between the TEF and the REF and recognize that teaching, learning and research are the core of much HE activity and should not be treated as though they are in competition with each other.

It appears that the separation of research and teaching may have some unintended consequences, and if seen in some ways as different activities, opportunities to benefit from the mutuality of research and teaching are lost. The commercialization, commodification and marketization of higher education (see Nixon, 2012) have influenced both institutions' strategic priorities and management practices to monitor the achievement of these. This is perhaps unsurprising, as Blackmore notes in connection with his discussion of prestige, 'every league table can increase or damage institutional standing, in an environment that is now global rather than national' (Blackmore, 2016: 67). It may be understandable, therefore, if the 'strategic positioning of staff' is an institutional response to such factors. The example drawn from higher education in Russia illustrated the influence exerted by global rankings and understandings of excellence.

Conclusion

This chapter has examined how higher education policies appear to have shaped institutions' perspectives on teaching excellence, with a particular focus on English universities. In turn, universities' articulation of teaching excellence has significant implications for their management and academic practices. The existence of separate frameworks for teaching excellence and research excellence may undermine the synergies and relationships between teaching and research. Such compartmentalization may also create silos within institutions and be divisive in terms of career trajectories evolving along discrete research or teaching pathways.

> ## Points for Discussion
>
> - Is the proportion of first-class and upper-second-class degrees awarded a good indicator of teaching quality?
> - Do universities genuinely provide equal career progression for both teaching- and research-focused academics?
> - Would academics perceive the same prestige for teaching-focused promotions?
> - How is teaching excellence conceived differently by higher education institutions in different national contexts? How much are their conceptions shaped by the higher education policies in their contexts?

3

Academics' Perspectives on Teaching Excellence

In this chapter, we examine academics' perspectives on teaching excellence in higher education. The chapter builds on a previous empirical study (Wood and Su, 2017) undertaken into academics' perspectives of teaching excellence as we explore academics' views of the term, examples of what excellent teaching might look like in practice and the issue of the measurability of teaching excellence.

While in the context of higher education in the UK there was some cautious optimism for the TEF, our findings showed that this was tempered by some concerns that the idea of 'teaching excellence' is beset by its opacity. Furthermore, there was a broad agreement that simplistic proxy measures impoverish understandings of this multilayered concept. Through metrics and rankings, institutions may attempt to demonstrate that they are 'hitting the target', but are they in danger of 'missing the point' when it comes to teaching excellence? In this chapter we argue that 'hard' data, which seems to speak with such a loud voice today, ought not to drown out the 'quieter' acoustic of non-numerical but vital qualitative aspects of teaching excellence. Questions are also raised in this chapter about the risk that an emphasis on measurement may distract attention from issues of how the development of teaching is resourced and supported.

What Contributes to Excellent University Teaching

Bain's study (2004) of teachers in the United States aimed to uncover 'what outstanding professors do and think that might explain their accomplishments'

(p. 4). 'Outstanding teachers' included in the study were those deemed to have had 'remarkable success in helping their students learn in ways that made a sustained, substantial, and positive influence on how those students think, act, and feel' (p. 5).

The study found 'an intricate web of beliefs, conceptions, attitudes, and practices driving the accomplishments of the best teachers and their students', and the strands of the web were interconnected; therefore, 'to understand what makes some teaching exceptional, we must know the individual strands and how they nourish one another' (p. 72). Outstanding teaching emerged as complex, labyrinthine and included intangibles such as appreciating the individual value of each student (p. 72), reflecting a strong trust in students and tending to treat students with 'simple decency' (p. 18). Furthermore, outstanding teachers strove to create the conditions of a 'challenging yet supportive' learning environment (p. 18). In such an environment, students feel safe to 'try, come up short, receive feedback, and try again' (p. 47).

Such findings point to some of the more abstruse aspects of an excellent or outstanding higher education practitioner, which, being also inherently subjective, appear to evade expression through outcome measures. O'Leary, Cui and French (2019: 13) have pointed to the difficulties when it comes to capturing aspects of excellence such as a higher education educator's personal attributes and the quality of the relationship with their students through measurement: 'despite decades of research, defining what makes an HE educator "excellent" can often cohere around their personal attributes and the quality of the relationship they have with their learners, both of which are notoriously difficult to measure in any empirical sense.'

Bain's study made clear that to try to convey the idea of teaching as if it is merely down to technique and procedures is too simplistic, for 'the best teaching is often both an intellectual creation and a performing art' (p. 174). Taking this view, there can be no toolbox of techniques to simply copy, nor any universal blueprint or script for teaching excellence which can be followed. As Boyd and Singer (2011: 60) noted, teaching excellence 'must be personally constructed and deconstructed based on a lifelong process of self-conscious, thoughtful reflection and interaction with our students – mirroring precisely the same "critical thinking" process we expect from those we teach'. This has synergies with Bain's (2004) findings that outstanding teachers 'can do intellectually, physically, or emotionally what they expect from their students'

(p. 16), being learners themselves, 'constantly trying to improve their own efforts to foster students' development' (p. 20).

Dixon and Pilkington's study (2017) examined the rise of excellence in the further education (FE) context and the resulting effects on its construction and measurement in two colleges in the North West of England. They have argued that, while excellence is portrayed as being first-class, robust and achievable by policymakers, on the one hand, there is a darker side, on the other. The findings of their study suggest that 'the teacher's voice within FE has been suppressed in constructing local definitions and enactments of excellence. The consequences include stress, changes in teachers' behaviour as a result of pressure to achieve, and unpredictability around teaching practice' (p. 447). It indicates that, as in higher education, teaching excellence discourse in the further education context is largely defined by policymakers. As a result, the teachers' teaching practice is potentially adjusted for performativity and measurement cultures.

Writing in the context of higher education policy in Australia, Cooper (2019: 89) noted the shared recent concern with teaching excellence in both the UK and Australia, which has emerged 'as part of the audit and quality improvement "turn" in higher education that commenced in the 1990s'. She observed that the ethos of competition emphasized in this policy context has brought with it an appetite to achieve recognition for teaching through teaching awards for staff. This is potentially divisive as individual excellent practitioners compete, and successful ones are championed and singled out; the 'awarded "heroes"' then become 'role models of excellence' and are marked out 'as different from the many other teachers who have not been selected or who have not applied' (p. 93). This, Cooper suggests, distracts attention from the systems that support teaching, including issues of decreasing resources and declining financial support for teaching:

> The process obscures the reality that a smaller share of resources is allocated per student to support teaching, which means that class sizes have been rising steadily for two decades (Bradley et al., 2008; Lomax-Smith et al., 2011; Universities Australia, 2013), and as student groups have become more diverse, preparation time has decreased, and student contact hours have declined. (Cooper, 2019: 94)

One step which Cooper suggests in her range of possible alternatives to the dominant managerialist approaches would be to use data to improve support systems for teachers and students rather than as a tool to monitor the performance of individual academic staff: 'This would require a change of assumptions to prioritise supportive systems over individual "heroes". This would provide better support for collaborative approaches to teaching and learning and for the formation of genuine communities of scholars' (p. 94).

This chapter builds on our previous study of academics' perspectives on teaching excellence (Wood and Su, 2017) and draws on empirical data gathered via interviews with seventeen academics from five English universities and a Music Conservatoire in England.[1]

How University Academics Understand the Idea of 'Teaching Excellence'

In the main, our participants appeared not to object particularly to the term 'teaching excellence', seeming in their thinking to connect it to ideas associated with the effectiveness of academics in enabling student learning, as in the following example where Participant 1, an Education Developer, suggested:

> It means achieving a level of competence in teaching which maximises students' learning gain and their capacity for original, critical thought, and which is recognised as an exemplary practice by peers.

A reference to peer recognition for this practice is apparent here, too, perhaps almost as a form of validation of teaching excellence. As illustrated in the following two selected quotes from Participants 5 and 3, respectively, both of whom were senior lecturers in Education, constructions of the excellent teacher conveyed the demanding and highly skilled nature of the role. It combines a knowledgeable reflective educator, a research-informed pedagogue and the necessary digital capabilities and interpersonal skills to ably plan, 'deliver' and assess student work:

> The term teaching excellence summarises the essence of good practice. The term encompasses the need for research driven and pedagogically informed teaching. It should be fundamentally relevant and up to date and should aim to have an impact on the student's knowledge and experience.

> [is someone] who has high levels of subject knowledge and command of the area, highly developed presentational skills with optimum use of technology (be it high or low tech), empathetic approach to the planning,

teaching, feedback and assessment, appropriate support material and quality reflection.

Interestingly, with regard to assessment, Bain's study found that outstanding teachers had a 'learning-based', in contrast to a 'performance-based', approach to assessment. The learning-centred approach appeared to reflect aspects of what Participant 3 may have been referring to as an 'empathetic approach' in that in a learning-centred approach they 'used assessment to help students learn, not just to rate and rank their efforts' (2004: 151).

> Rather than asking if the student said anything in class or did a certain assignment and made a certain score, the professor asks what we will call the fundamental assessment question: What kind of intellectual and personal development do I want my students to enjoy in this class, and what evidence might I collect about the nature and progress of their development? (Bain, 2004: 152–3)

Participants also recognized some indefinable aspects which are understood and experienced in affective and emotional senses, as seen in the comment from Participant 7, a principal lecturer in Education:

> An excellent teacher ought to leave the students feeling something positive and, in some way, fulfilled.

Some participants drew attention to tricky issues in employing the term 'teaching excellence' due to a lack of shared agreement about what it means and therefore being open to a myriad of possible interpretations. Therefore, as Participant 14, a lecturer in Biology, indicated, disconnects between these interpretations are possible:

> Student expectations of excellence may not be the same as staff. Students might misinterpret this as expecting a high level of support (hand-holding) whereas staff may feel it facilitates students in developing their higher level skills and fosters independent learning.

Participant 9, a professor of Educational Research, suggested another term they would prefer instead.

> I disliked and have always disliked the term 'excellence'. It is overused, forms part of every rhetorical statement about education and now is almost meaningless. Even before when it did mean something I would have been

very hesitant about using it, as it has to be a rare and exceptional quality – how can we all be excellent? I would prefer a word like 'dedicated'.

As for the pertinent question raised by this participant, namely 'How can we all be excellent?', not all excellent teachers can be excellent all the time. Bain (2004: 19) noted that 'Even the best teachers have bad days, as they scramble to reach students. As the study revealed, they are not immune to frustrations, lapses in judgment, worry or failure. They do not even always follow their own best practices. Nobody is perfect.'

The lack of clarity about the term 'teaching excellence' may be a factor in the sort of misinterpretations referred to by Participant 14. As reported in the literature, teaching excellence is poorly defined. The Centre for Higher Education Research and Information (CHERI) report (Little et al., 2007: 4), for example, noted: 'At a national level, there needs to be much clearer explication of the precise meaning being attached to the term "excellence" to ensure that given the UK's diverse higher education system, certain (more traditional) notions of excellence are not implicitly privileged over others.' More recently, in reviewing definitions of teaching excellence in the literature, Bartram, Hathaway and Rao (2019: 1285) identified 'a widely reported lack of consensus on a commonly agreed definition of teaching excellence'.

The student expectations of excellence referred to by Participant 14 may also be linked to the idea of students as consumers and paying customers and to the commodification of culture (Shumar, 1997: 5). Through commodification, market value predominates and 'eventually the idea that there are other kinds of value is lost' (Shumar, 1997: 5). Shumar discusses how 'the process of commodification has changed public institutions and affected individuals at those sites' (p. 11).The 'misinterpretation' referred to by Participant 14 may be related in part to the influence of processes of commodification on conceptualizations of excellence and student expectations. Shumar suggested that 'Universities are busily developing and putting to work technologies of consumption; developing ways to get people to *buy* courses, programs, degrees, certificates and ideas' (Shumar, 1997: 5).

A 'technology of consumption' may promote buyer–provider relationships, influencing student expectations of their roles as customers and their relationships with academics. This discourse contrasts with the academics' conceptualizations, which appear to be more reflective of understandings of excellence where value is ascribed to higher education in other ways.

Academics appear to emphasize the value to excellent teaching of relations which are construed in terms different from those used in technologies of consumption. For example, in the aforementioned quotes our respondents ascribed value to empathy, dedication and facilitating students' development. These appear reflective of what Shumar (1997), as discussed earlier, referred to as other kinds of value, which are lost in the process of commodification.

Examples of Excellent Teaching

Due to the complexities and contested nature of teaching excellence, asking participants for illustrative examples was not a straightforward request, as they explained. Participant 8, a senior lecturer in Computing, felt that

> It is quite difficult to give specific examples of excellence in teaching if you take the view that it is a complex and holistic concept. Any examples inevitably omit things, otherwise you end up with *War and Peace*.

For some, it was almost intuitive, rather like a case of 'you know it when you see it'. For example, Participant 10, a senior lecturer in English Literature, cited an occasion when teaching generated excitement and stimulated interest which continued after the formal lecture session had finished.

> I remember watching a former colleague lecture on structuralism and hearing students coming out of the lecture hall discussing ideas and raising questions as soon as they were leaving the building, which emphasised to me that they had taken something significant out of the room where the teaching was actually taking place.

Examples of teaching excellence were not seen as 'spoon-feeding' or teaching that cast students in passive roles. Excellent teaching allowed students to develop independence as learners. As Participant 1, an Education Developer, illustrated with reference to an experiential, enquiry-based approach to learning:

> it required a 'letting go' by the tutor so that students could discover and create new knowledge as researchers with some degree of independence; and it was linked with knowledge retention by the students.

'Letting go' may mean allowing students freedom to learn from mistakes. This may not be 'satisfying learning', but it is an important part of higher education.

Excellent teaching with this purpose in mind appeared to be reflected in the following response, in which the idea of 'dedication' and the dedicated teacher mentioned earlier by Participant 9, are illustrated further by this same participant:

> A dedicated teacher makes the fear of learning manageable and provides a safe space for the student to make mistakes, so that failing is seen as learning and growing.

This requires the excellent teacher to balance challenge and support carefully; as Participant 9 explained, an excellent teacher is one 'who supports a student through periods of self-doubt while still challenging them to do it again, do it better, persevere until the student is successful'.

One characteristic of excellent teachers referred to by participants is that they draw on data, such as student feedback, to inform evaluation and development of their practice. For example, one participant referred to 'evaluation leading to appropriate and innovative development/evolution of their teaching practice' (Participant 4, a professional tutor in Health). Interestingly, Bain's (2004) study of what the 'best' teachers do noted the importance to them of 'constantly trying to improve their own efforts to foster students' development, and never [being] completely satisfied with what they had already achieved' (p. 20).

Participant 10, a senior lecturer in English Literature, argued for the importance of gathering students' feedback after they have completed the whole degree course, as this may indicate some of the more enduring aspects of excellent teaching over a longer term:

> Student feedback after graduation is one of the most powerful indicators, for me, of whether teaching has achieved excellence. Memorable, transformative, impactful learning experiences leave a mark that lasts longer than an end of course evaluation.

Issues of Measurement and Teaching Excellence

Measuring something as complex and intricate as teaching excellence in a way which does it justice was considered very problematic. Participant 5, a senior lecturer in Education (in the first extract), and Participant 9, a professor of Educational Research (in the second extract), suggested that measures were simplifications, a form of reductionism, which merely capture contributory factors.

> The pure essence of teaching excellence is often difficult to pinpoint. It goes hand-in-hand with the desire to make a difference. To feel we have a positive impact on those we teach. This is very difficult to actually measure.
>
> We can measure proxies of teaching excellence only, we cannot measure or reduce to what is measurable the complexity of the learning teaching encounter.

Measures can only be 'markers' or 'pointers' towards an idea that is much more involved and elaborate, and as such 'any metrics are difficult to identify that will capture the richness of excellence' as Participant 8, a senior lecturer in Computing, remarked.

Participants' views suggest our gaze must extend beyond metrics if we are to appreciate the complexities and subtleties of excellent teaching. Another dimension to this is what the metrics purport to measure and how adequate and meaningful they are considered to be. Anxieties were expressed by some that the drivers for teaching excellence were political, for accountability purposes and to drive market competition in higher education. They had some concerns that teaching excellence may become reduced to evidence-gathering. For example, Participant 2, a senior lecturer in Education, considered that 'This is just another example of the accountability agenda being taken too far in the current neoliberal climate!' and Participant 3, a senior lecturer in Education, remarked:

> The TEF is simply another example of a rhetoric about quality, choice, rigour which is anything but. At best it is an attempt to get universities to focus on the student experience and produce quality outputs; at worst, it is a stick to beat higher education with. Teaching quality can be calibrated but qualitatively not quantitatively. In terms of measurement, it should be possible to capture the features, describe them and use them as a guide to make judgments that have a shared currency. Again, I think this is only part of the story, which should be about learning.

While recognizing contentious and problematic issues with TEF, many participants appeared hopeful in anticipating the prospect that it might raise the profile of teaching and enable it to have a similar status as research. However, this was tempered with caution regarding the pressures of a culture of consumerist expectations, as illustrated in the words of Participants 9 and 1, respectively:

In spite of all its obvious limitations, I welcome it in the sense that it raises the status of teaching, but I fear it will never have the same prestige as research; however, to the individual dedicated teacher, that would not really matter.

Whilst I have serious reservations about the terminology and measurements/metrics surrounding teaching excellence, I welcome the prospect that the status of teaching will be raised in research-intensive institutions. I hope that the renewed focus on teaching and students will encourage a less individualistic culture amongst academics in HE; however, I also hope that 'what students want' is not taken as what ought to be done. I also hope that research and teaching are not pitted against each other, since good research should lead to good teaching.

Overall, some of the key messages that appear to be raised by this data concern both the lack of clear understandings of teaching excellence and its subjective aspects; these may be described through qualitative data but are obscured when measures of excellence are reliant on quantifiable 'hard' data. Yet, at the same time as having reservations, many participants welcomed the opportunity TEF may offer to raise the status of teaching and its parity with research. O'Leary, Cui and French (2019: 7) also found that 'understanding, recognising and rewarding excellent teaching in HE is an important undertaking that is welcomed by staff working across HE provision', although on the basis of the evidence from their study, they still strongly suggested that the TEF failed to capture teaching excellence in any meaningful way (p. 83).

Notwithstanding an optimism regarding the prospect that the TEF may raise the profile and status of teaching in higher education, our participants also expressed concerns that teaching excellence was serving a political agenda, and they noted that teaching excellence is only 'part of the story', which is also about student learning. The marketization of higher education and the influence of the development and enactment of 'technologies of consumption' by universities (Shumar, 1997) has been drawn on to contrast the apparent dissonance between academics' conceptualizations of teaching excellence and the commodification of higher education. The academics' views were often infused with terms which appeared at odds with a view of higher education operating within and regulated according to a set of market relations. The data evidences beliefs about teaching that emanate from a different discourse and an alternative view of value and purposes. Excellent teaching may not necessarily aim to provide learning that is always 'satisfying', either. Learning may be unsettling with no clear-cut ready-made answers, but higher education is about creating educated students rather than satisfied customers, as we discussed in Chapter 1 with reference to the work of Saunders and Blanco Ramírez (2017).

Our respondents expressed a concern that what students want should not automatically be taken as what should be done, as seen for example in the 'you said, we did' approach which is sometimes adopted as a way of responding to student feedback. Instead, our data evidenced a different orientation to that of higher education as a technology of consumption. This orientation was signalled in their ideas of excellent teaching as facilitating students' learning and as 'letting go', thus allowing students to become knowledge discoverers and creators, freeing them to make mistakes and to learn from these.

Teaching Excellence in Other Higher Education Settings – A Music Conservatoire Setting

The thoughts of a UK Conservatoire Principal (Participant 17) are drawn on in this section to contribute a perspective on teaching excellence from a relatively small specialist institution which is a higher education provider. Course provision includes undergraduate degree courses with a focus on music and performance. This adds to our thinking and awareness of the different lenses through which conceptions of excellence can be viewed in a diverse higher education sector. In such a diverse sector, we may expect views of excellence and, in the UK higher education context, sentiments towards the TEF, to differ. Furthermore, as noted earlier in this chapter, drawing on Boyd and Singer's (2011: 60) work, teaching excellence is 'temporally and spatially contingent'. The sector includes higher education providers that are relative 'newcomers', alongside incumbents with greater longevity. There are different kinds of 'providers' of higher education in the UK as part of a government drive to create a diverse competitive system offering different types of higher education from which students can choose (BIS, 2011: 47 para. 4.6). Insights from a Conservatoire setting enrich our thinking about what teaching excellence might mean in the specificities of different locales and remind us of the diverse nature of higher education across a wide heterogeneous sector.

In 'Success as a Knowledge Economy: Teaching Excellence, Social Mobility and Student Choice' (BIS, 2016: 43 para.7), it is recognized that 'excellent teaching can occur in many different forms, in a wide variety of institutions', and therefore it is illuminating to consider how teaching excellence is perceived and interpreted in a Conservatoire context. At Conservatoires, 'all courses have a strong vocational, performance orientation, and course structures are reflective of the industry'; 'the year is broken down into a block of academic weeks, followed by a block of performance weeks'; and 'all teaching staff at conservatoires are working professionals. There is a strong emphasis on one-to-one tuition, alongside group work and performances' (Universities and Colleges Admissions Service (UCAS) Conservatoires).

The thoughts of the Principal (Participant 17) were shared during an interview, the purpose of which was to explore ideas about teaching excellence from a senior leader in a Conservatoire setting and a provider of higher education. The conversation took the form of a rapport interview, which sought to uncover 'depth and roundedness of understanding' (Mason, 2002: 65) and insights into perceptions of teaching excellence as experienced in the particularities of this context. In addition to the questions asked of our other participants, the Principal was also asked, 'How does the Teaching Excellence and Student Outcomes Framework (TEF) affect your institution, and in what ways?', and 'If you were invited to advise the government on the reform of the TEF, what would you like to suggest?' The data offers a contrast in capturing the views of a senior academic leader and a Conservatoire setting.

Higher education study in this setting employs a number of teaching strategies. These include one-to-one tuition for students with professional experts, a highly valued teaching method in the Conservatoire and used 'because it is proven to have an enormous impact on our students in an excellence context' (Participant 17). Collaborative group work is also used to offer opportunities for peer-to-peer learning. Through use of a range of teaching and learning strategies, students 'equip themselves for the composite career of a music professional' (Participant 17). Opportunities for students to learn and collaborate together have particular importance in a Conservatoire environment, as this participant explained:

> One of the drivers of excellence [then] in a Conservatoire context is actually not the quality of teaching at all, it's the quality of the other students and that's really important in institutions like this – ateliers like this – it's how the student

next to you is excelling and driving you further and motivating you further, and we see evidence of that in ensemble environments and so forth. That is probably one of the absolute hallmarks of what a Conservatoire might be.

Therefore, in this context teaching excellence is thought of in relation to a range of strategies which include both the professional expert and apprentice model alongside peer-to-peer learning. The Principal explained that 'You are learning more about yourself through your peers as much as you are through teaching' and the concept of teaching excellence in a setting such as this is directly related to the quality of peer learning.

Yet, while the driving forces for excellence in musicianship in this Conservatoire learning environment are bound up closely with collaborative peer-to-peer learning, we note from Brink that 'With the TEF we are talking about the teaching provided to students, not about any growth in their learning. The TEF is not a Learning Excellence Framework. The problem with this is that teaching is not an end in itself. Teaching is but a means towards an end, which is learning' (Brink, 2018: 138). Hanken's discussion of peer learning in specialist higher music education (2016) noted the emerging evidence of the value of peer learning, which can benefit students and complement their learning within a one-to-one teaching context (p. 372). How other students are excelling is an important and distinctive catalyst for the quality of learning interactions in the ensemble environment. In this environment, complex processes of peer collaboration between musicians appear central to a culture of excellence. Gregory (2010: 395–6) conveys a clear sense of the intricacies of the multifarious and intangible processes at work:

> Collaboration is about connecting with people, their context and the culture it creates at a particular moment in time. For participating artists, especially playing musicians, it is about accepting a bond, accepting everything for the way it is. It takes a lot of patience and a lot of taking chances with each other. It means seeing each other in weak and strong lights, accepting both and utilizing the high and low points of the relationship. Above all it transcends the qualitative and the quantitative.

In terms of employability, too, 'Being creative and being a multifaceted performer effective in collaborative environments are important qualities for musicians who want to remain employable' (Gregory, 2010: 395).

Among the key points that emerged from the data was an understanding that peer-to-peer learning was seen as centrally important as a driver of excellence alongside the one-to-one specialist music teaching by expert professional musicians.

Nixon (2007: 22) has suggested that 'Excellence is a process of growth, development and flourishing; it is not just an endpoint.' However, in reality, the Principal perceived that 'the pendulum has swung towards a very instrumental view of the education system', which is narrow and omits more abstract, impalpable considerations of the wider purposes and value of education, and they wondered:

> what is lacking so far from the discussion, [is that] the discussion seems to be around the price of everything and the value of nothing. And so the value piece is, you know, what is the value in a democracy of allowing young people to pursue all of these . . . whatever their desire, [whatever their] ambition looks like, even if it's in an area that doesn't fit easily into the productivity challenge, what is the value of that in a democracy?

In Chapter 1 of this book, teaching excellence and matters of cost and value were discussed. This perspective from a Conservatoire context adds to our thinking about more intangible aspects of value, including, for example, the cultural value that the work of musicians and artists adds to society, the importance and impact of which is not necessarily shown in terms of graduate outcomes. This suggests the need for a clarion call for new thinking about the dominance of measurement, productivity and matters of value perhaps, in the light of the TEF as these words from Participant 17 appear to indicate:

> The question is around cultural value. Can that be measured? . . . Why are the creative arts and humanities important? . . . If we don't have really, really robust thinking about the value that this creates for society then it is going to be very vulnerable, and it is currently very vulnerable within the outcomes side of the TEF, graduate earnings, Destinations of Leavers from Higher Education (DLHE) data, all of these things. I think that the public good argument will look radically different in say 30 or 40 years' time, where the robots will be doing lots of jobs. So lots of things that we currently understand as 'excellent' within the TEF, because they deliver great graduate earnings and thus support repayment of loans etc., you know the sun is going to set on those industries over the next 20 or 30 years.

This participant mused that the world of the artist and creator may then come to the fore. The future may be 'a time of crisis and challenge, but also opportunity and renewal . . . and if you look at the course of history, these are times when the idea of the artist in society has great importance'.

Important challenges are posed for education and democracy when excellence is conceptualized narrowly and only in terms of relevance, productivity, efficiency and cost effectiveness. It seems an opportune time to rethink teaching excellence and to frame it to factor in wider considerations which include the value of higher education in a democratic society. This raises some profound and interesting questions, as the experiences in this setting suggests. A capacity for originality and creativity, cultural value to society and the cultural and artistic heritage of the country appear vulnerable. While the reference here is to the Conservatoire setting, the implications appear to be far wider.

Implications of Academics' Perspectives on Teaching Excellence

The language for 'teaching excellence' is problematic and politicized and, as discussed in Chapter 1, as a term it is blurry, ambiguous and often contested. A range of understandings, meanings and emphases exist as to what constitutes excellence in the higher education context. Our study has revealed academics' awareness of the limitations inherent in a discourse of 'teaching excellence' which is open to myriad interpretations and understandings, and a concern that the discourse of excellence may become reduced to an empty rhetoric. Our interview with the Conservatoire Principal has provided some insights into how teaching excellence is interpreted and practised in the context of a specialist higher education provider.

Our respondents' accounts evidenced something of the complexities and intangible aspects of teaching excellence, which may be considered impossible to quantify by measurement. Academics were aware that the use of proxy measures and a reductivist focus on what can be evidenced in a tool such as the UK TEF fail to capture the subtleties and complexities of the teaching and learning processes. The TEF's slavish attachment to outcomes neglects the importance of process and the 'richness of excellence' cannot be conveyed adequately in simplistic proxy measures. Furthermore, measures do nothing to support the development and improvement of teaching excellence. Arguably too, measures of teaching excellence need to recognize the influence on outcomes of systemic issues such as support, resourcing of higher education, the influence of marketization and the funding regime. Therefore, as noted at the start of this chapter, an emphasis on measurement ought not to distract attention from issues of how the development of teaching is resourced and supported. As we discussed earlier, a similar point was made by Cooper (2019: 94) in Australia, regarding the ethos of competition and focus on individual excellent practitioners distracting attention from decreasing levels of resource and financial support for teaching. Measurement was seen by respondents as a feature of the 'neoliberal climate' of higher education, which was also highlighted by Cooper (2019) in her discussion of New Public Management and how it has influenced thinking about public services and engendered a competitive environment.

Competition in rankings is now a preoccupation for the sector and the stakes are high, for example, in terms of the reputational damage inflicted by low rankings. Rankings assume significance and exert considerable influence, having a number of different users and possible consequences; for example, as Hazelkorn (2015: 25) discussed, institutional resources may be directed to areas that shape prestige, and governments and institutions may use rankings to guide the restructuring of higher education. However, arguably measures and rankings tell only one 'part of the story'. As Hazelkorn noted, 'Because of the difficulties identifying and agreeing meaningful reliable and verifiable international comparative indicators and data, rankings measure what is easy and predictable, concentrate on past performance, and emphasize quantification as a proxy for quality' (p. 89). Cooper (2019) identified tensions between marketization and the purposes of higher education. The issue of measurement may align with considerations of efficiency, cost and quantification, but when it comes to matters of value and purpose, it appears that, as one of our respondents commented, there is a need to apply more robust thought. Rankings and measurement may drive behaviours and raise a concern that teachers' teaching practices potentially could be adjusted for performativity and measurement cultures, as we noted with reference to the work of Dixon and Pilkington (2017).

For teaching excellence to flourish, it appears that certain conditions need to be present. From Bain's (2004) study we come to appreciate that excellent teachers create the conditions of what Bain refers to as a 'natural critical learning environment', where learning is embedded in intellectually stimulating, authentic and intrinsically interesting tasks which foster a spirit of curiosity, and where students develop as critical thinkers (p. 99). The perspectives of respondents in our study mirrored some aspects of Bain's findings, for example, the importance of creating 'safe' learning spaces where students feel able to try, make mistakes and learn from these as one of the hallmarks of excellent practice. These conditions may be strengthened by empathy, honesty and openness – shown, for example, when teachers discuss with students the challenges that they have sometimes experienced themselves as learners. Such honesty and openness can be supportive for students when they are also experiencing difficulties in their learning. For example, Bain (2004: 18) noted that highly effective teachers 'often display openness with students and may, from time to time, talk about their own intellectual journey, its ambitions, triumphs, frustrations, and failures, and encourage their students to be similarly reflective and candid'. These conditions appear to play a positive role in fostering students' desire to learn.

Furthermore, from Cooper's (2019) work, the importance of support for the conditions to develop collaborative teamwork approaches to teaching and learning emerged. This was contrasted with the competitive marketized environment of Australian higher education; in such a competitive environment, collaboration and teamwork are undermined. In Cooper's critical analysis of the development of teaching quality in conditions of a decline in organizational support and dwindling funding, the contradictions and tensions were apparent, and an argument was made for the necessary conditions for responsive teaching to be established (Cooper, 2019). In a UK Conservatoire setting, although not exclusive to this, we noted the importance of creating learning conditions to support collaboration among students. This emerged as a central contributor to students excelling as learners. Collaborating as musicians and motivating one another can drive the quality of learning and achievements, and in this atelier environment one of the ways teaching excellence was conceptualized was in relation to the quality of student peer-to-peer learning.

Some elements of the conditions needed to develop teaching excellence are 'intangibles'. Fullan and Hargreaves (1996: 18) remind us that 'teaching is not just a collection of technical skills, a package of procedures, a bunch of things you can learn', as has become evident in this chapter. 'Intangibles' may include the 'dedication' referred to by one of our respondents, an 'empathetic approach' referred to by another, and other aspects which, as a further respondent noted, are the 'essence' of teaching excellence but are hard to pinpoint. Fullan and Hargreaves (1996: 18) observed that 'Teaching is not just a technical business. It is a moral one too.' We glimpsed this, for example, in the words of one respondent who felt that excellent teachers leave students feeling something positive and with a sense of fulfilment, and that such things evade 'hard' data capture. In similar ways to Fullan and Hargreaves, Bain (2004: 174) also put forward that it is simplistic to think that good teaching is all down to technique.

In addition, staff–student pedagogic partnership ways of working enable knowledge about excellent teaching to be co-constructed, as we examine further elsewhere in this volume. Such approaches reflect commitments to equity and the value of the experiences and perspectives of academics and students to co-create knowledge about teaching. Co-constructing knowledge about teaching excellence engages and combines the diverse perspectives of staff and students. The benefits of combining and connecting lived experiences and bringing university academics' views of teaching excellence into dialogue with student perspectives is a theme explored in Chapter 4 and revisited in the Coda.

Conclusion

Teaching excellence has emerged from the foregoing discussion as multi-layered, complex and nuanced. As Boyd and Singer (2011: 60) noted, 'There is no single, best way to teach and no all-inclusive model for what constitutes teaching excellence.' In a performativity culture in higher education today, where targets, outcomes and measurability dominate, then ostensibly, according to this discourse, excellent teaching becomes evidenced when targets are hit. But as we suggested at the outset, in hitting the target we may also be missing the point when it comes to teaching excellence. Managerialism and a climate of competition, in which teaching excellence becomes reduced to an evidence-gathering process, appear in tension with support for the conditions needed to rebalance and restore the importance of qualitative aspects discussed in this chapter.

Some of the layers and nuances of teaching excellence have been made apparent in this chapter, including, for example, the importance of cultures of co-operation and systems and resources to develop and sustain it, and the relationship between teaching excellence and student peer-to-peer learning. Academics ascribed value to constructions of teaching excellence which appear at odds with market-led understandings, and tensions were seen in the imperative for high levels of student-consumer satisfaction and the purpose of higher education to develop educated citizens.

Points for Discussion

- How do academics' perspectives on teaching excellence differ from those of other stakeholders'?
- What are the implications of the dominant discourse of teaching excellence for academic practice?
- How do academics negotiate the tensions between performativity culture and academic freedom?
- Is it possible for academics to be excellent in both research and teaching? What are the potential barriers to achieve excellence in both areas?

4

Students' Perspectives on Teaching Excellence

This chapter examines the idea of teaching excellence as understood by students and considers its significance for higher education. It draws on current research and our previous study on what students perceive as teaching excellence and its implications for academic practice (Su and Wood, 2012). If we regard students as an important stakeholder group in higher education, then it is crucial to include understandings of their expectations and what these might mean for the development of teaching excellence.

In this chapter, we begin by examining the positionality of students, and we establish the value placed by students on the quality of lecturers as central to any conception of teaching excellence. This is followed by an analysis of secondary data on students' conceptions of a good university lecturer. The discussion in this chapter juxtaposes the contrasting discourses of what we have referred to as students as customers/consumers and students as partners. At the end of this chapter, we examine the limitations of the student-consumer concept, which arguably diminishes the role of active learner participation and engagement.

Students' Positionality and Teaching Excellence

Bunce, Baird and Jones (2017) discussed the influence of marketization and the consumer identity of students at universities in England since the introduction of tuition fees and found that a 'higher consumer orientation was associated with lower academic performance'. Among the practical implications arising from their findings, they suggested the value of universities beginning a dialogue with students about the student-as-consumer approach and its consequences; they also suggested that 'governments and universities should resist conceptualizing students as consumers in the first place. By drawing attention to concepts like "value for money" this may inadvertently encourage students to view their education as an exchange of money for services' (Bunce, Baird and Jones, 2017: 1973).

In contrast to the customer/consumer identity is the discourse of students as partners. Healey, Flint and Harrington (2016: 2) suggest that 'Partnership is a specific form of student engagement, with very high levels of active student participation. Partnership is a way of doing things, rather than an end in itself.' Their model of students as partners in learning and teaching in HE identifies four overlapping areas in which students can be partners in learning and teaching: learning, teaching and assessment; subject-based research and inquiry; scholarship of teaching and learning (SoTL); and curriculum design and pedagogic consultancy. Of these four, 'engaging students actively in their learning is the most common form of partnership' (p. 3).

Unlike a student customer discourse, a partnership approach positions the active engagement of students and their roles in knowledge construction in learning at the forefront. Central to the teaching excellence framework is the NSS score, which therefore does give prominence to the idea of student voice in the debate on teaching excellence in some ways. However, it can be said that the idea of the student as consumer limits the value placed on students as partners in their learning and therefore externalizes the responsibility of teaching excellence primarily on the educator. In good university teaching, alongside the prominence of factors such as subject expertise, pedagogic capability, good communication skills and skills in digital technologies is the relationship between tutor and student and the climate for learning. These emerge as part of the alchemy that helps to explain some of the intricacies of excellent teaching. A learning relationship thought of as a learning partnership is qualitatively different from that between consumer and provider. The positioning of students in the development of teaching excellence appears ambiguous. The 'consumerist turn' in higher education and the 'consumerist levers' (Naidoo, Shankar and Veer, 2011) which can be utilized by students sit uneasily alongside more democratic practices based on the principles of co-construction. These ideas are teased out further in this section.

The chapter began with a brief consideration of the wider discourse of 'student-as-consumer' linked to the marketization of higher education and the juxtaposition of this with the 'students as partners' discourse. Regarding the positioning of students as consumers, Naidoo, Shankar and Veer (2011: 1142) note that 'The ascendance of market mechanisms in higher-education systems worldwide has led to the conceptualization of students as consumers of higher education.' Universities now operate in a competitive market; competition is seen as a driver for improvement and as a mechanism to promote value for money for consumers. Higher education has taken a 'consumerist turn' (Naidoo, Shankar and Veer, 2011), and a number of 'consumerist levers to enhance student choice and control over the education process have been introduced in the international context' (Naidoo, Shankar and Veer, 2011: 1145). Continuous evaluation of their higher education experience and teaching quality from students is now commonplace in HEIs. For example, as mentioned previously, in the UK context, the National Student Survey (NSS) has become an important tool to ensure that higher education is responsive to student demands and to assure their satisfaction. The impact of the NSS on universities in the UK has been significant and 'powerful' and has been exacerbated by the 2016 introduction of the UK Teaching Excellence Framework (TEF), which partially utilizes NSS data to then allocate a 'gold, silver or bronze award' to universities' (Thiel, 2019: 539).

In a Quality Assurance Agency (QAA)-funded study, Kandiko and Mawer (2013) 'explored the views of students in higher education across the UK in 2012–13, to investigate their expectations and perceptions of the quality of their learning experience and the academic standards of their chosen programmes of study' (Kandiko and Mawer, 2013: 6). The research team interviewed over 150 undergraduate students at sixteen institutions in the UK, and a major finding from the study was that

> dominant across all student year groups, institutional types and subjects, students have a consumerist ethos towards higher education, wanting 'value-for-money'. This was seen tangibly through sufficient contact hours and resources available and abstractly through institutions' investment in students, learning spaces and the educational community. (p. 7)

On the quality of teaching, they found that

students praised enthusiastic, experienced and engaged staff, but wanted mechanisms in place to develop staff and to manage 'bad' teachers. Students wanted staff to be qualified and trained, and students expressed a desire for procedures to manage 'bad teaching', described as lecturers not knowing the course material, reading off slides and failing to offer any support to students. . . . [S]tudents complained about academics who ostensibly took the attitude of 'just doing their job'. Students wanted lecturers who were passionate and knowledgeable about their subject, with sufficient content knowledge and teaching capability. (pp. 10–11)

One of the aspects which appeared favourable in the case of two of the institutions receiving Gold awards, as reported by Beech (2017) in an analysis of a sample of provider TEF submissions, was staff–student partnerships; this suggested that 'demonstrating staff–student partnerships may be a successful strategy to enhance perceptions of teaching quality' (p. 25). Within the neoliberal context, the juxtaposition of concepts of students as consumers with students as 'co-creators' and 'partners' is an uneasy one. Naidoo, Shankar and Veer (2011: 1145) envisage the likelihood that 'the grafting of a framework derived from the commercial sector onto a sector with a deeply imbedded professional culture that is still steered by the state may not translate easily into the outcomes intended by policy makers.'

In this policy context, the student's role in the development of teaching excellence appears to serve different purposes. A market rationale assumes that teaching excellence is furthered through pressure from the consumer, that is, the students, and the choices they exercise in the higher education competitive marketplace. As Wood and O'Leary (2019: 117) suggest, developments in teaching excellence in England evidence a system that has 'moved away from engagement with the situated meaning, process and complexity of teaching, towards a metrics-based system that relies on the use of questionable proxies that neither focus on the student (other than as consumer) nor the academic (other than as supplier) in a meaningful way'.

Healey, Flint and Harrington (2016) note that 'Students as partners is a "hot" topic internationally' (p. 1) and 'a rapidly growing area of interest in higher education' (p. 9). Learning and working in partnership can be seen as an alternative to consumerist models of HE, a point apposite to our foregoing discussion. Healey, Flint and Harrington (2016: 9) suggest that 'Students as partners is a concept and practice whose time has come. Co-creating, co-producing, co-learning, co-designing, co-developing, co-researching and co-inquiring involve sharing power and an openness to new ways of working and learning together and, hence, challenges traditional models of HE relationships.' This appears at odds with a competitive, marketized higher education sector and a TEF where the onus is on the teaching provided to students (Brink, 2018). In the context of the TEF, O'Leary, Cui and French (2019: 70) found that 'institutional systems and policies were increasingly framing interactions and communications between academic staff and students in a way that encouraged staff to "treat students as consumers"'. This appears antithetical to democratic approaches to teaching excellence and the discourse of 'co-creation'. Dollinger and Mercer-Mapstone's (2019) examination of the terminology used to conceptualize the changing roles of students in higher education is instructive and relevant to this discussion. Dollinger and Mercer-Mapstone's work includes a dialogue between the authors in which some critical thinking is exchanged about the potential for co-option of the idea of students as co-creators within a neoliberal view of student engagement rather than functioning as an idea that contests neoliberal aims (2019: 80). For example, the point is made that 'Emphasis on listening to your students' preferences and their individual voices could be both situated within a neoliberal rationale that results in the enhancement of services at the university (e.g. Dollinger, Lodge and Coates, 2018) and seen as a means to achieve social justice or legitimation of student voices' (p. 81).

Healey, Flint and Harrington (2016: 1) note that 'Recent research indicates that pedagogic approaches that foster partnership lead to supportive learning relationships and employability benefits for students.' Trowler's (2010) review of the student engagement literature points to the ideological roots of this concept within constructivism. As a theory of learning, constructivism is grounded in an active part played by the student in learning which arguably is somewhat at odds with a consumer orientation. According to constructivist understandings, teaching is about 'engaging students in active learning, building their knowledge in terms of what they already understand' (Biggs and Tang, 2011: 22). Jensen, Adams and Strickland (2014: 38) maintain that 'The literature shows that it is essential for excellent teachers to not only know their subject very well, but also have a keen interest in how learning happens and how knowledge is constructed.' It can be argued that focusing narrowly on teacher performance and outcome measures as evidence of teaching excellence lessens the emphasis on the centrality of the role of the students in their learning.

Teaching Excellence and Quality of Lecturers

Recently, a consortium of students' unions in the UK commissioned a survey study on students' perspectives on teaching excellence (2017). Over 8,990 undergraduate students from 123 higher education institutions participated in the study. When students were asked which factors most demonstrate that a university has excellent teaching, the quality of teachers was considered to be the most significant. Lubicz-Nawrocka and Bunting's study (2019) also concurred with this view that students' perceptions of teaching excellence are largely influenced by their perceptions of the quality of teachers. They identified four themes which were perceived by students as important: concerted, visible effort; commitment to engaging students; breaking down student–teacher barriers; and stability of support offered. In a study of undergraduate students' conceptions of excellent teaching, Mimirinis (2020) also found that excellent teaching is about the optimal presentation of the subject matter; about being taught by an excellent teacher; about enabling and achieving an understanding of the principles of the subject matter; about questioning knowledge; and about bringing about change in the discipline.

This chapter builds on our previous study of undergraduate students' perceptions of a good university lecturer and teaching excellence in the context of the UK higher education (Su and Wood, 2012). The qualities of university teachers appear to be pertinent for improving students' learning. The secondary data set analysed in our previous study indicates that students' conceptions of teaching quality and what makes a good lecturer appeared to be informed particularly by their own direct learning experiences with academics at the course level. Our research bears some similarities with the themes reported in Lubicz-Nawrocka and Bunting's work. Within the themes we have identified, qualities such as enthusiasm and the ability to inspire are important to student engagement in learning. As acknowledged in one of the narratives our study drew on, the role of good teachers is to 'light the match' rather than 'fill the bucket'. The narratives emphasize the importance of the energy and effort invested by lecturers in 'lighting the fire'. Words and phrases such as 'upbeat', 'packed a punch', 'teaching that leaves you with a rush' and 'nothing was too much trouble' communicate a strong sense of the energy and effort involved on the part of the tutor and the support provided to 'guide in the right direction'. In the next part of this chapter we turn to findings from this previous study in more detail.

Students' Perspectives on Teaching Excellence

Teaching excellence is a contested concept (Bartram, Hathaway and Rao, 2019: 1285). The concept is elusive and subjective (O'Leary, Cui and French, 2019: 13) and invoking the term 'good' here as an alternate is considered appropriate and not out of kilter with the use of terminology in some of the literature on teacher/teaching excellence. In their discussion of excellent teaching and inspirational teaching and issues of definition, Jensen, Adams and Strickland (2014) noted that terms are often used interchangeably and most literature on teaching quality in higher education uses terms such as 'good practice', 'excellence' or 'effectiveness' to refer to similar conceptions of teaching practice (Jensen, Adams and Strickland, 2014: 37).

Being Able to Apply Knowledge to Real Life Scenarios

There was evidence that students expected that the good lecturer would be highly qualified and would have specialist subject knowledge and pedagogic expertise. The ability to forge links in their teaching between theories and real-world relevance was referred to, as in the following account from Vanessa, a third-year student studying Human Services:

> A good lecturer equips his/her students with a range of tools to be adept in this subject and to be able to see the relevance of it. So in my opinion the most important quality in a social science lecturer is the ability to link the academic theories with real life and to be able to see every side of an argument. They also need to be able to put their own personal beliefs to one side to allow the students to be able to find their own position in the discussion.

Putting aside personal beliefs and focusing on enabling students to think through their own stance, as suggested in this quote, implies that value may be attached here to pedagogical approaches that encourage students to discuss and think for themselves rather than one-way didactic approaches with the tutor positioned as knowledge provider/giver and students as recipients.

In terms of 'linking academic theories with real life', as mentioned previously, case studies are an example of a useful means to make these connections. Healey (2011: 201) recalled what he described as an 'ah-ha' moment when realizing the value that incorporating mini-case studies into guides to teaching, learning and assessment had added, by involving and engaging colleagues in learning. This stimulated awareness that in the same way, case studies might act as a useful tool to engage students with learning:

> We incorporated many mini-case studies in the guides. In running some of the workshops I quickly learnt that my colleagues were far more interested in the case studies than they were in the principles and theories which underpinned their application. This was an 'ah-ha' moment for me, as I realized that if this was how my colleagues were engaged, 'what about my students?' Since then I have usually started my sessions with case studies and later introduced theories and concepts to help interpret them. (p. 201)

An illustrative example of the value of incorporating case studies was suggested by Warren, a third-year student studying Engineering:

> Equally engaging are lecturers that discuss real-world case studies such as the collapse of a particular structure, the design of a working radio, the selection of materials for a 400-ton aircraft. One I found particularly stunning was when a lecturer described the structural failure of a pipe in a cyclohexane plant, and demonstrated that any first year engineer could have spotted the initial pipe's design flaw. What is that famous saying, again? A case study is worth a thousand words?

Making learning accessible is important, and students also commented on teaching which was stimulating, challenging and enjoyable, too. For example, as Emily, a third-year student studying Disability Studies, referring to the impact of such teaching on her learning experiences, commented:

> At the university, I experienced the type of teaching that leaves you with a rush. Questioning everything. Teasing out beliefs about the world, values, preconceptions and attitudes. Shaking your sense of reality. Not sitting

comfortably in your chair. So, it is safe to say that I really liked the learning and teaching experience during my undergraduate degree. What did I like about it so much? Mostly, I liked the way the teaching packed a punch. The way in which content was delivered gave a strong sense that the theory, research and information we absorbed really mattered in a real-world context. We – the students – knew it mattered because our tutors shared stories from their own lives and practice, whilst encouraging us to draw upon our own subjective experiences. Often, I remember that a personal story told by a tutor or student was a pivotal moment in helping to make a theory 'click' in my mind. The understanding that disability studies theory and research matters in real-world contexts was a strong impetus for my engagement with and enthusiasm for the degree. The lectures given as part of my degree often carried undertones of rallying calls for activism. When you feel part of a movement that is challenging social oppression, it's hard not to pay attention.

While to some extent uncomfortable and challenging, it appears that at the same time by 'packing a punch' teaching can be stimulating and powerful when students develop a strong sense that the learning has importance and that it matters. As we have noted elsewhere, not all learning is satisfying; nor does it always provide neat, clean answers. The sentiments expressed by this student invoke Bain's idea of excellent teachers having 'a sustained, substantial, and positive influence on how students think, act, and feel' (Bain, 2004: 5), through those 'pivotal' moments to which the aforementioned student referred. Pivotal moments could be when students experience some kind of a learning breakthrough, perhaps aided by occasions when a tutor shares something of himself/herself through personal anecdote. The influence on how students 'think, act and feel' is clear in words and phrases such as 'strong impetus for engagement', 'enthusiasm', and feeling a connection, which create engagement and even a spur to action. Such aspects are difficult to capture in the measures demanded by dominant consumerist conceptualizations of teaching excellence. As Bartram, Hathaway and Rao (2019: 1287) note, 'methodologies for measuring excellence are thus becoming a key focus, as institutions are increasingly expected to provide evidence of the quality of their teaching'.

Being a Good Communicator

It appeared that students identified a good lecturer as having a range of skills. These included communication skills and skills in the use of educational technologies, together with interpersonal skills and qualities, including a sense of humour, an approachable and accommodating demeanour, an ability to engage students in learning and being reflective practitioners, as we will discuss further. In the following extract, for example, Nicholas, a third-year student studying Information Technology, refers particularly to communication and to being friendly and approachable:

> Good people skills are a virtue to be had for a good lecturer. Being able to communicate ideas effectively is essentially the whole point of lecturing! It would therefore make sense that a person be able to convey facts and thoughts to a classroom, in a friendly, approachable, and generally good-natured manner. This will pay off for both parties, since students will be more likely to pay attention to somebody they can respect, and as a result they should have no qualms in questioning certain areas they may not understand so well.

This narrative appears to suggest the importance of approachability among the 'people skills' in the lecturer's repertoire so that students feel able to seek further support in areas of learning that may not be easy to understand. While being a good communicator is important, good teaching 'is about much more than having the capacity to stand before a classroom full of students, speaking coherently, advisedly, seamlessly and with humour' (Hay, 2011b: 209–10). Approachability and the importance of a sense of humour are themes that emerged from our analysis of the students' narratives, as we examine next.

Being Approachable

Being approachable was regarded highly in terms of its importance for a good lecturer. Approachability means that lecturers are available, accessible, make time to explain and with whom students feel confident to ask for further explanation when needed, as illustrated by Lara, a fourth-year student studying Engineering:

> Accessibility of the lecturer outside of class time is also an invaluable student resource but rarely found. One such lecturer who gave up his time by making a conscious effort to be in the student coffee shop inspired my learning more than anyone else. For him nothing was too much trouble and he was ready to

engage at every level, be it first year or PhD. With him I never felt belittled or intimidated by asking the same question twice or even going back to basics. If I did not understand his explanation using one example he was always ready with another approach. For me this is at the heart of excellent teaching.

Having a Sense of Humour

Having a sense of humour was regarded by a majority of students as being important for a good lecturer, as illustrated by Nicholas, a third-year student studying Information Technology, in the following:

> Making students laugh should definitely be applied as an aid during the lecture. It not only takes some off [sic] the pressure off the host, but additionally acts as a minor interlude during what may be an unavoidably dull session of Blah for the 4th time in as many days. Injecting a bit of humour into the mix always tends to lighten the tone, and laughter is supposedly said to act as a memory trigger, which could even enhance the learning of material by simple association.

Being Good at Using Educational Technologies

Educational technologies are typically used in teaching and assessment in higher education, and students appeared to expect a good lecturer to utilize learning technologies to aid their learning, for example, as Victoria, a first-year student studying Computer Science, suggested:

> Nowadays, most lectures are given as PowerPoint presentations. The good lecturers take advantage of this, not only using it for text but also diagrams, images and videos to help explain the point they are trying to put across. Handouts are useful so that the students do not have to frantically transcribe everything the lecturer is saying and merely need to add notes to the information that is already there. From my experience, I have found that the odd witty cartoon (relevant or not) inserted on a slide in the middle of a presentation is guaranteed to hold my concentration.

With the growth in the use of digital technologies in learning, online and blended learning, Massive Open Online Courses (MOOCs) and so on, then arguably the skills and capabilities of the e-pedagogue are now important to support e-learning as well as more traditional learning face to face.

Being Able to Interact with Students

For many students, a good lecturer interacted with them, asked for their opinions, invited their questions, ignited imagination and facilitated student peer-to-peer interaction. For example, Siobhan, a third-year student studying Modern Foreign Language and Sociology, suggested:

> The next feature is almost always neglected in lectures: facilitating interaction between lecturer and audience and amongst the audience themselves. Having appealed to students' imagination, you must allow them an outlet for it! Many teachers no doubt think this unnecessary in large lectures, leaving it to seminar tutors to listen to the students' ideas. But let me ask you: having lit a firework, would you shut it in a room? Or would you release it into the open air? Use what you have created; exploit the tension by demanding a display of quick thinking; show your respect for students' opinions by asking them to contribute, even if only briefly. The students will feel honoured and the respect will be reciprocated, encouraging them to take precious note of your every word.

This quote appears to point to the importance of pedagogical skills to facilitate interactions, teaching that appeals to the imagination and the creation of a classroom climate that is respectful of students and their learning.

An important idea latent across the data set was also that of student engagement with learning. Harper and Quaye (2009: 2–3) suggest that 'Student engagement is simply characterized as participation in educationally effective practices, both inside and outside the classroom, which leads to a range of measurable outcomes.' Students appeared to prize the lecturer who can engage them with the learning in a host of different ways. A particular alchemy of turning arid, sterile material into something interesting and memorable, for example, involves a range of pedagogic strategies in the repertoire of the educator. Passion and inspiration are important, too, and are referred to again later. These factors appear significant in the estimation of students in creating engagement with learning.

Being Passionate and Inspiring

Students considered that good lecturers would have a passion for their subject, they 'light the match', helping to make their lectures inspiring and stimulating further learning, as suggested in the words of Dave, a third-year student studying Sociology:

> It's got to be a passion for the subject and an urge to share that with others – to get other people to be as interested in it as you are. No-one likes being 'lectured' – a good 'lecturer' is someone who doesn't make it feel like a lecturer! It ought to be about exploration, illumination, and curiosity. Good lecturers 'light the match' – inspiring you to go and find out more. Bad lecturers try to 'fill the bucket' and just load you with information. If you set out with the right intentions, the mode of delivery, the use of interaction, visual aids etc. all follow – attitude is paramount, skills develop as a result of trying to do something better.

In their examination of inspirational teaching, Jensen, Adams and Strickland (2014: 37) found that 'Inspirational teaching as a theoretical or analytical term is little used in the literature on higher education; it is mostly associated with personal awards in the field of teaching and learning. The inspirational teacher, however, remains a powerful image or concept.' They identified four overarching themes in the literature as constituents of inspirational teaching: knowledge and passion for the subject; understanding learning and knowledge; constructive and challenging learning environments; and students as individuals, partners and colleagues. However, they argue against reducing inspirational teaching to a set of characteristics or practices.

Good lecturers find ways to trigger enthusiasm, even if that subject happens to be not that exciting. As Nicholas, a third-year student studying Information Technology, suggested:

> For a lecturer to be passionate about the subject they teach is arguably the greatest trait of all. For instance, a lecturer I had a few years ago would usually append each learning outcome with how this section we had just covered was 'the single most truly beautiful thing ever'. It was fantastic to see a lecturer genuinely enjoying what he was doing, and passing on his knowledge of that field to a new generation. I have to be honest though, at the time I struggled to find the material THAT beautiful . . . but I definitely appreciated it far more than if the lecturer had not been such a character! His upbeat attitude was hugely encouraging. I had never experienced this kind of atmosphere in a lecture before. I'm certain his passion for the subject brushed off on me and others, which vastly enhanced my learning experience.

Being Supportive and Able to Provide a Safe Space for Students

This appeared to overlap to some extent with aspects of 'approachability'. Students considered that a good lecturer would appreciate the difficulties students may face in learning and would offer as much support as possible. One of the important aspects of being supportive is through creating a classroom culture that is experienced as a safe space for students to make mistakes and to develop their understanding. As Melanie, a first-year student studying Social Work, noted:

> The environment of the seminar group feels safe. When we start to talk about new ideas, there is always (for me) that moment when I fear I am going to make a fool out of myself, or discover that I have huge prejudices I had never reflected upon before that have been made apparent through discussions about social exclusion or entitlement. In my group, it feels OK to make those mistakes; they generate debate, and seem to be the most effective method of challenging discrimination I have seen on the programme so far.

Being Able to Facilitate Students' Independent Learning

A lecturer may use strategies to guide and encourage each student's learning and independent follow-up work, and Warren, a third-year student studying Engineering also refers to how the lecturer drew on students' ideas and suggestions and used them to improve the lectures.

> Some of the best lecturers I have had are not stand-up comedians, intent on making semiconductor engineering hilarious, but on the contrary they are people that give students a chance to develop and learn by guiding them in the right directions, adding links to interesting web-pages in handouts, posing interesting challenges in lectures. One of my lecturers encourages creative thinking and independent learning by handing out chocolate bars to students who find and email him interesting applications/articles/anecdotes that relate to the electromagnetics course, which he can then show other students and use to improve his lectures.

Being Able to Provide Timely and Quality Feedback

Timely, helpful feedback on assignments is also appreciated by students and can aid progress. However, this is not always the case, as Lara, a fourth-year student studying Engineering, noted:

> Lecturers who return assignments in a timely fashion, or indeed at all, are to be credited. Even better is to receive your work marked but also with valuable comments, constructive criticism or suggestions for improvement. It is extremely disheartening in my experience to spend many hours and sleepless nights on an assignment only to find the cursory 'collect your work from the pile at the front' and only an illegible grade scrawled at the top. Lecturers need to get us to aspire to excellence but how can this be if we are treated in such a mediocre manner? I have to add at this point that once I had reached my dissertation in the third year I was in truth given more attention but sadly many students had already fallen by the wayside and whatever engineering potential they once showed is lost forever.

This student felt disheartened by some experiences of receiving feedback on an assignment and, this appears relevant to Ramsden's (2003: 187) observation that

> It is impossible to overstate the role of effective comments on students' progress in any discussion of effective teaching and assessment. Students are understandably angry when they receive feedback on an assignment that consists only of a mark or grade.

Ramsden (2003: 187) also suggested that 'It seems that beneficial information about progress is valued even more by students than qualities such as clear explanations and the stimulation of interest.' This reinforces the importance of feedback on progress and raises awareness of the sentiments experienced by students when feedback is deemed inadequate. Ramsden (2003) sees assessment as part of teaching and learning and as being concerned with

> reporting on students' achievements and about teaching them better through expressing to them more clearly the goals of our curricula. It is about measuring student learning; it is about diagnosing misunderstandings in order to help students to learn more effectively. It concerns the quality of teaching as well as the quality of learning; it involves us in learning from our students' experiences, and is about changing ourselves as well as our students. (Ramsden, 2003: 177)

This helps to explain the importance of assessment feedback for the quality of student learning and its role in excellent teaching. The extract demonstrates that feedback comments with suggestions for further development were valued. It also shows that 'cursory' and inadequate feedback practices can be 'disheartening' and it appears to be implied that this may be a factor when some students 'fall by the wayside'.

The aforementioned findings point to the need for a good university lecturer to possess several different abilities and attributes and also to the need to reflect on their practice as a form of professional development, as explored in the next section. Students' reflections on what makes a good university lecturer show some overlap with Skelton's (2007) conceptualization of four perceptions of teaching excellence: traditional excellence emphasizes mastery of knowledge and logic within a disciplinary area; performative excellence highlights individuals' abilities to excel in employment; psychologized excellence focuses on students' development of deep learning skills; and critical excellence aims to empower students to participate as critical thinkers who question knowledge.

Being a Reflective Practitioner

Biggs and Tang (2011: 45) suggested that 'Expert teachers continually reflect on how they might teach even better.' In fact, the term *'Transformative reflection'* is preferred because as they explain: 'When you stand in front of a mirror what you see is your reflection, what you *are*. Transformative reflection is rather like the mirror in Snow White: it tells you what you *might be*' (2011: 45). Theory has an important part in transformative reflection, as they discuss, and 'Reflecting on your teaching, and seeing what is wrong and how it may be improved, requires an explicit theory of teaching' (2011: 45). In the following, Caroline, a third-year student studying Linguistics, appears to point towards the role of self-reflection and the importance of empathy.

> A good lecturer is a good student. He is able to examine the pupils in front of him, and address his lecture to their needs. He may have progressed in years and understanding far beyond the youthful faces in front of him, but he must always remember the difficulties he himself faced at their stage, the things which aided his comprehension, and most importantly the gems which inspired him to go on to academia: he must pass these on, not only for the sake of the students, but also for his own sake, for those listening intently to him today may be the ones who will go on to carry the torch for his field in the next generation.

Reflective practice is de rigueur in many professions, including teaching, and seen as making an important contribution to professional development:

> Use of reflective practice is now so widespread across a range of professions that it has almost become clichéd. Yet it has the potential to

be a powerful support for professional learning and development. (Forde et al., 2006: 66)

The student implies the importance of empathy on the part of the tutor to help build bridges with the students' learning. Being a reflective practitioner, able to reflect back on their own learning experiences, may aid in this.

Implications of Students' Perspectives for Advancing Understandings of Teaching Excellence

Wood and O'Leary (2019: 115) have noted that 'As the HE sector in England has become ever more commercialized and marketized, so too has it become increasingly reliant on accountability systems and the use of metrics for both research and teaching.' It is not uncommon nowadays in the market environment in which universities operate to see terminology and concepts which seem to be more congruent with the commercial and business world being employed in university mission statements, strategic plans and policy documents. In this marketized environment, we hear the student referred to in terms of a 'consumer'. As Naidoo, Shankar and Veer (2011: 1142) have observed, 'The ascendance of market mechanisms in higher-education systems worldwide has led to the conceptualization of students as consumers.' To cast the student in the role of consumer suggests a limited view of student learner engagement, although arguably one which the developing marketization of higher education appears to endorse.

We have contrasted the student-as-consumer discourse with that of the discourse of the engaged student. The latter is seen as an active participant in learning and contributing to excellent teaching; the former is associated with the role of a passive consumer of education, which in turn is conceived of as a 'product' received or 'purchased' from a 'provider'. Naidoo, Shankar and Veer (2011: 1150–2) discuss some of the consequences of a student-consumer identity in promoting narrow conceptions of their role as learners and make contrasts with a model of co-creation.

A focus on teaching excellence can divert attention from student learning, and yet '"Teaching excellence" is about making learning happen well. It's really about *learning excellence*' (Race, 2005: 66), and as Ramsden (2003: 7) suggests, 'the aim of teaching is simple: it is to make student learning possible.' Ramsden

(2003: 6) argues that 'we can improve our teaching by studying our students' learning – by listening to and learning from our students.' Students' views of teaching excellence are important and need to be listened to and learnt from, as are the perceptions of academics and other stakeholders. Arguably, conceptualizations of teaching excellence are richer and more meaningful when established in partnership with students. However, in the UK context and in relation to TEF, O'Leary, Cui and French (2019) reported that 'While there was a consensus on the importance of student voice, there was also the recognition that it needed to be balanced with the inclusion of "staff voice", which many felt was currently neglected' (pp. 77–8).

On the basis of the data set on which we have drawn, broad generalizations for the wider body of undergraduate students are difficult to make. However, some interesting themes emerge which have points of connection with themes in the literature. The relationship between tutor and student appears central to achieving teaching excellence. The inspiration, the excitement and the enthusiasm which appear to promote student engagement are interlinked with the relationships the tutor creates with the students and which in turn help to set the tone and climate for an excellent learning experience.

Conclusion

In this chapter, we have argued that students' perspectives on teaching excellence appear to be shaped significantly by their own direct learning experiences with academics at course level (as also evidenced by Lubicz-Nawrocka and Bunting's study in 2019). Alongside considerations such as specialist subject expertise, understanding how students learn, pedagogic capability, communication skills and feedback on progress, students appeared to value the qualities of enthusiasm, approachability, humour, passion for learning, responsiveness to students' interests and support for their learning needs. How important qualities such as energy, inspiration, passion, for example, are nurtured and enabled by lecturers in a dominant managerialist culture in higher education is a question that has emerged from our research. In the UK context, O'Leary, Cui and French's research (2019: 63) reported that 'the TEF had created another layer of administrative bureaucracy, which had given rise to additional workstreams, often with no additional resources to support this extra workload' together with increased stress anxiety and low staff morale (p. 64). Arguably these sorts of factors may serve to undermine some of the vital aspects of teaching excellence evident in our study of students' perceptions. In highlighting students' conceptions of a good university lecturer, we have argued for the value of listening to students' views and recognizing their role as partners and important stakeholders in informing any contemporary and future debates on the development of teaching excellence. Developing an inclusive perspective on teaching excellence requires a commitment to listen to and learn from multiple student voices reflective of the diverse nature and experiences of the student population. Building inclusive understandings of teaching excellence therefore requires engagement with the views of a broad constituency of students. Partnership approaches that 'simply engage already engaged students' (Bovill, 2020: 39) may thereby fail to engage certain other voices. Bovill's reminder that '. . . care needs to be taken to ensure genuine engagement is possible in a range of different ways and at different times by all students, but particularly underserved students' (Bovill, 2020: 39) is apposite to our call for inclusive perspectives on teaching excellence.

The Black Lives Matter uprising brings new emphasis to well-established struggles and injustices and demands a re-examination of institutions and their practices, bringing a new focus to the debate. While the book was in preparation, this was brought to the surface and raised questions about some of the data that is available and the potential for inbuilt cultural biases. We recommend that examining students' views of teaching excellence becomes a genuinely inclusive exercise and note that this is an issue we wish to highlight. One of the consequences of this fresh emphasis on examining the adverse impacts of colonialism and its continuing effects is how this points to an issue of inbuilt biases. If there is a commitment to examining teaching excellence, then there is a need to ensure that this is an inclusive approach. Growing awareness through public debate, political action and educational response highlight the continuing and negative legacy of colonialism on culture, ways of thinking and practice. The need to be open and inclusive, to recognize the myriad ways the legacy and influence of colonialism pervade and shape practices and policy and the implications for the development of teaching excellence are things to be borne in mind for people doing work in this area.

> ## Points for Discussion
>
> - In what ways has the marketization of higher education shaped students' expectations for their university learning experience?
> - How do universities consider students' well-being in their pursuit of teaching excellence?
> - What active roles might students play in improving university teaching quality?
> - Does teaching excellence focus too much on teaching rather than the role of learners and learning?

5

Employers' Perspectives on Teaching Excellence

This chapter explores employability in higher education and, drawing on data from an empirical study, examines employers' perceptions of how well undergraduate courses develop graduates' readiness for the world of work and how this relates to teaching excellence. Judging the quality of teaching through graduate-level employment outcomes raises a number of issues and tensions which are examined in this chapter, for example, between employability and the wider purposes of a university education. Questions about the relationship between graduate-level employment outcomes, the economy and labour market conditions, skills for employability and the quality of teaching are also examined. A push for skills acquisition in curriculum design may favour more vocationally oriented subjects, marginalizing and devaluing many of the wider benefits of other non-vocational subjects (see Carasso and Locke, 2016). The discussion in this chapter points to the need for a wider debate about teaching quality and the purposes of higher education to include employer organizations and other stakeholder groups, an idea that is developed further in the final chapter.

University Education and Graduate Employability

There is some apparent confusion over the distinction between employability and employment. These are not the same thing; indeed, as McCowan (2015: 270) has noted, 'While employability is often gauged through employment, the two concepts are clearly distinct.' Rich (2015) defines employability as 'the ability to get, keep and succeed in jobs you want – both now and in the future as the economy shifts'. A university may do well in developing graduate employability, but 'the problem universities face is that there is not necessarily a correlation between employability and employment' (Slane, 2017).

'Employability' has importance for universities worldwide: '"Employability" may be a British term, but the concern with higher education's contribution to the graduate labour market is international' (Knight and Yorke, 2004: 1). Norton (2016: 155) has argued that 'The whole purpose of university education is constantly shifting, and at present, the indications are that universities are rapidly becoming training grounds for employment rather than seats of learning'. The issue of what stakeholders see as the purposes of university education is relevant to our discussion of employability and teaching excellence. The focus of the chapter is employers' perspectives, but as Norton also notes, 'Students and their parents expect the cost of a university degree to be recompensed in the form of improved chances in the labour market' (p. 155). Findings from the UK study by O'Leary, Cui and French (2019) evidenced the key focus on 'employability' in many institutions in course revalidation and review, and reported in their findings that 'Participants repeatedly mentioned the increasing "pressure to embed employability skills into modules", which was a particular challenge for those subjects where there is not a clear vocational pathway' (p. 67).

Drawing on a range of international studies, O'Leary notes the growing importance of the issue of graduate employability in higher education internationally (2017: 85). This is a concern for universities worldwide, including the UK in the context of the TEF, part of the rationale being as a way of 'better meeting the needs of employers, business, industry and the professions' (Department for Education, 2017: 6).

The term 'employability' is understood in different ways; often, it denotes skills beneficial for employment, including what are sometimes referred to as 'soft skills', as we explore in the following selections from the literature. In their critical examination of the TEF and the policy context, Barkas et al. (2019: 807) suggest that 'Employability is broadly a notion that implies that a university should offer a set of learning outcomes or skills to its students that on graduation will make them more attractive to employers.' Støren and Aamodt (2010: 298) view it as 'the benefit and usefulness of the study programme for career and work tasks'. Yorke (2004a: 422) argues that '"Employability" is a complex construct, under which many aspects are subsumed' and also that 'there are many interpretations of "employability"' (Yorke, 2004b: 5). Yorke uses the following working definition of employability: 'a set of achievements – skills, understandings and personal attributes – that make graduates more likely to gain employment and be successful in their chosen occupations, which benefits themselves, the workforce, the community and the economy' (p. 7).

McCowan (2015: 267) has suggested that 'Employability is becoming increasingly central to the mission and functioning of universities, spurred on by national and supranational agencies, and the demands of marketization.' Cole and Tibby (2013: 9) note that in the last twenty years, the trend has been towards 'graduate attributes', which have included 'softer' skills. Given the increasing centrality of employability to universities (McCowan, 2015), there is often an ambition to embed employability in the curriculum and opportunities to gain experience in work settings through periods of placement. Employability is not limited to skills, and neither are the benefits only for employment: 'Despite the name, "employability" can be understood as a concern with learning that has benefits for citizenship, continued learning and life in general' (Knight and Yorke, 2004: 8). Minocha, Hristov and Leahy-Harland (2018: 246) suggest that there is more to be done in terms of ensuring that graduates are equipped with 'the right *kind* and *level* of skills and attributes to succeed in a globally-competitive employment market'. As well as valuing good academic qualifications, employers expect students to have well-developed employability skills (Saunders and Zuzel, 2010).

Lowden et al.'s (2011) research found an expectation on the part of employers of graduates having both 'technical and discipline competences from their degrees' as well as requiring evidence of graduates having 'broader skills and attributes including team-working, communication, leadership, critical thinking, problem solving and managerial abilities' (vi). Their research showed that in terms of promoting employability, importance was given to work-based learning. On the basis of their findings, Lowden et al. (2011) recommended encouraging HEIs and employer partnership activity and employers playing a more active role in HEI employability strategies and policies (p. viii). Furthermore, it appears that employer participation could be more significant: 'Employers' presence on HEI committees should not be a token measure but allowed to facilitate a meaningful contribution. Our study found that employers' views on course design were often disregarded' (Lowden et al., 2011: viii).

Lowden et al. (2011: 25) recommended that degree course design should be informed by partnership with employer organizations, without compromising 'academic quality, content, focus and the "integrity" of courses'. The research suggested that in exploring alignment of types of degree course provision and the requirements of the wider economic climate, this should be with the caveat that higher education learning should also address broader social issues and needs (Lowden et al., 2011: 25).This proviso is important, for while 'increasing pressure to meet the expectations of stakeholders has driven the employability agenda and made it a priority in the 21st century for all higher education providers' (Advance HE, 2016), arguably the aims and purposes of higher education are not defined solely by one stakeholder group's needs. Furthermore, the purposes of higher education are not limited to meeting the needs of business and the economy, for as a public good, higher education provides 'the goods necessary to become full and rounded human beings in every aspect of our lives' (Nixon, 2012: xii) and, it could be argued, able to contribute and add value to civic society.

We begin with a brief examination of some of the reasons why graduate employability appears to have been a topic of growing interest over the last decade (Lowden et al., 2011: 4) and a concern to the fore on the higher education agendas of governments both in the UK and across global higher education (Minocha, Hristov and Leahy-Harland, 2018). This is linked to the idea of the knowledge economy, based on the notion of knowledge as central to economic competitiveness and that 'better educated nations would have an edge in the global economy' (Lauder et al., 2012: 1). Education is seen as a worthwhile investment in the knowledge economy, being linked to increased earning potential, an idea which can be expressed in the equation 'learning=earning' (Lauder et al., 2012: 2). However, this premise appears not to be matched in reality, as we discuss shortly with reference to massification and the knowledge economy. Higher education institutions today are global businesses (Williams, 2016: 202). Changes to the financing of higher education have passed the financial burden onto individual students as customers, who in turn have expectations of a return on their investment in terms of future earnings. Today's graduates may expect to work for longer and to retire later than previous generations. However, the world of work may well look very different in the future. Brown, Lauder and Ashton (2012: 9) note that while the extent varies according to national context, 'All affluent nations are witnessing the growth of a high-skill, low-wage workforce.' Robotics and automation have implications for employment in the future, including for skilled occupations (see Ford, 2016). The issue of job–education mismatch is raised when considering the future world of work and the nature of the labour market.

Job–education mismatch, defined as 'a lack of correspondence between the qualification level the job requires and the qualification level the employee has acquired through higher education (vertical mismatch)' (Støren and Aamodt, 2010: 298), is relevant when considering the issue of the graduate premium. The graduate premium is an idea which 'has time and again been cited by spokespeople from successive governments, both left and right-leaning, as some kind of guaranteed bonus that all graduates will gain by taking on ever-increasing debt' (Kemp-King, 2016: 5). However, there is arguably a Faustian resonance to contracting to incur considerable debt in exchange for the promise of future gain via a graduate premium. Increasing numbers of graduates in turn leads employers to raise the bar in terms of the level of qualifications needed by prospective applicants, resulting in

> a self-perpetuating upward pressure on young people to get ever more qualified, therefore having to take on ever more debt in order to set themselves apart from other applicants. As more people become graduates, is it any surprise that previously low-to-median paid jobs now demand graduate-level qualifications? Not on any required intellectual level, but just because graduates are available, in huge numbers. (Kemp-King, 2016: 37)

It is to the supply of graduates, the 'massification' of higher education, the needs of the economy and the availability of graduate-level jobs that our discussion now turns. The implications of recourse to graduate employment data as a proxy measure of teaching excellence are discussed.

Massification refers to the process by which mass higher education is achieved (Tight, 2019: 94), and Tight reports that all higher education systems in the developed world, and many of those in the developing world, now provide mass higher education (p. 104). Similarly with reference to massification, Altbach, Reisberg and de Wit (2017) noted the dramatic change seen in higher education, which was once restricted to an elite social class, to a situation where 'gross enrollment ratios (the participation rate for the cohort between 18–24 years of age) in postsecondary education have mushroomed to more than 50% in many countries' (p. xii). 'Science, technology and innovation, the cornerstones of the knowledge-based economy, are now clearly on the agenda of both developed and developing countries, as fundamental to achieving sustainable development across the globe' (George, 2006: 607–8). Striving for teaching excellence when measured in terms of employment outcomes may have the effect of narrowing the curriculum to subjects such as STEM (Science, Technology, Engineering, Mathematics), which are prized in the knowledge economy for competitive advantage and attractive to consumers seeing education as an investment in future earning potential. As Lauder et al. (2012: 1) noted, a premise underlying the knowledge economy idea was that 'if individuals invested in their education and ascended the credential ladder they could secure well paid, high status jobs, in which creativity was at a premium'. The prevailing belief was in knowledge as central to economic competition, and thus 'better educated nations would have an edge in the global economy. Underlying this assumption was the view that the knowledge economy would usher in an increasing proportion of well paid, 'knowledge' jobs' (Lauder et al., 2012: 1). However, the issue of supply of graduates and competition for jobs suggests that the reality is somewhat different and more nuanced:

> While the 'official' account of the knowledge economy assumes a linear relationship between education, jobs and rewards, where mass higher education is predicted to reduce income inequalities as people gain access to high-skilled, high-waged jobs, the reality is more complex. In the USA and Britain the expansion of higher education has been associated with an increase in wage differentials (Mishel et al., 2007). This is not only between university graduates and non-graduates but within the graduate workforce.
> (Brown, Lauder and Ashton, 2008: 139–40)

In both affluent and emerging economies the supply of college-educated workers has expanded, and 'Even when limited to affluent societies, this expansion poses a problem because widening access to a college education lowers the value of credentials in the competition for jobs' (Brown, Lauder and Ashton, 2012: 7). Tight (2019: 98) noted the significant concerns expressed as to 'whether the increasing number of graduates being produced by higher education could all gain graduate level jobs, reaping the financial rewards for their investment and that of their government (a related trend here is, of course, the shift of financial responsibility from the state to the individual student)'. As discussed previously, the idea of a graduate premium may be something of a chimera.

To sum up, this section has noted that expectations of the prospects of obtaining graduate-level employment may not be matched in reality as opportunities appear limited in the labour market, with 58 per cent of graduates in the UK being in non-graduate or lower-skilled jobs (Minocha, Hristov and Leahy-Harland, 2018). Given the shift of financial burden for education from the state to the student (Tight, 2019), students may understandably aspire to realize a return on their investment in higher education in terms of graduate employment prospects. Some of the implications of graduate employment data being used as a proxy measure of teaching excellence have been noted and will be developed further in subsequent sections of this chapter. Discussions about employability often appear to centre on skills, as we examine in the next section, which argues for understandings of employability to go beyond a discourse of skills development to include what it contributes to *higher* learning in a higher education. This forms part of the discussion in the next section, in which data from our own small-scale qualitative research study[1] of employers' perspectives is drawn on.

Skills Discourse

Several themes emerged from our data regarding what employers look for from university teaching in readiness for the world of work. It was apparent that in addition to degree subject knowledge, 'skills' were looked for when employers recruit graduates, including 'soft skills' and attitudes towards work. The skills needed to manage relationships with clients, a professional attitude and standards of behaviour, together with communication and IT skills, are examples of these. Stewart, Wall and Marciniec (2016: 276) make the following differentiation between 'soft' and 'hard' skills. Hard skills are 'technical, tangible measurable competencies' and soft skills are 'those non-technical competencies associated with one's personality, attitude, and ability to interact effectively with others'. For employability, soft skills are valued by employers as much as hard skills (ibid.), something mirrored in our findings, too. In fact, as Stewart, Wall and Marciniec (2016: 277) note:

> When faced with deciding between two candidates with similar backgrounds, hiring managers agree that the candidate with soft skills

experience would have an edge over the other candidate with little to no soft skills competencies. From an employer perspective, soft skills competencies are necessary in order to remain competitive especially in a global world.

The skills of communication, problem-solving and critical thinking are examples of 'soft skills' and as expressed by one of our respondents, these are crucial in the business world. Stewart, Wall and Marciniec (2016: 276) indicate that 'many employers consider job candidates' **soft** skills as critical for professional success as traditional **hard** skills, especially in today's global marketplace' [words emboldened as shown in original text]. In fact, a focus on soft skills as having a crucial role for 'employability' was a prominent idea evident in our data. Respondents told us that in graduate recruitment what are often looked for are attitudes and soft skills such as initiative, an ability to relate well to customers, reliability, time-keeping and team work.

An employability business partner participant reflected on the fact that employers often prioritize graduates' character, attitude and soft skills over their technical knowledge, echoing points made by other respondents. Adding to the discussion of soft skills, a senior academic and business consultant recognized the role of the development of criticality and soft skills in the context of higher education and also pointed out the problems of teaching and measuring these:

> These [soft skills] are critical thinking, creativity, communication and collaboration. These core skills are hard to teach and measure, but they are skills that are crucial in business and the world of work.

Employers' Perceptions of Graduate Readiness for the World of Work

Despite the impetus in the sector to embed employability skills in the curriculum, there appeared to be a perception among some participants that graduates are insufficiently prepared for the world of work. For example, a senior careers adviser participant noted that

> Evidence from organizations like the Institute of Student Employers suggests that many employers consider new graduates to be under-prepared for the labour market when they leave university.

Foundation degrees are an example of academic learning applied to the workplace and the need for cooperation between higher education and employers. As McKenzie and Schofield (2018: 316) explain, 'designed as a two-year, usually vocationally based HE qualification, employer engagement was integral to the development of Fds [Foundation degrees] and a condition of validation (QAA, 2010)'.

As Little (2005) noted, the foundation degree programmes were 'meant to be designed both to be work-related and employer-focused, and to provide progression opportunities to an honours degree' (p. 139). Other examples of work-based learning include placements and longer-term internships. Little (2005: 144) suggested that time would tell whether foundation degrees would fill employers' needs for 'people who have both good technical and practical skills and who can bring a broader business awareness and personal skills to the work role, across a wide range of employment sectors'. Little was prescient in noting that 'if substantial numbers of students do in fact choose to use foundation degrees to progress within higher education rather than move into the labour market, then these new qualifications will fail to establish their distinctiveness and status in the labour market generally' (p. 145). In reality, progression to a full degree appears a popular option (McKenzie and Schofield, 2018: 317).

Our respondents indicated that employability is linked to the benefits of social and cultural capital, as seen, for example, in access to opportunities for valuable internship experience. One respondent, a careers adviser, referred specifically to the issue of social capital:

> In my view, generally undergraduate courses do not deliver the desired competencies. If a graduate has these skills, it is more because of their own social capital or initiative rather than their undergraduate courses.

Social capital is one of Bourdieu's forms of capital and a reference to

> all those social connections and networks that bring the old adage of 'not *what* you know but *who* you know' to the fore, as social contacts can open doors and ease the way for accessing different social positions and opportunities that might not be open to those agents lacking such elevated levels of social capital. (English and Bolton, 2016: 56)

Bourdieu (1986) maintained that 'The volume of the social capital possessed by a given agent thus depends on the size of the network of connections he can effectively mobilize and on the volume of the capital (economic, cultural or symbolic) possessed in his own right by each of those to whom he is connected' (p. 249). Some students will have more ready access to the social contacts and connections that can 'open doors', that is, enable access in terms of valuable and prestigious internship and placement opportunities, than others.

A senior academic and business consultant respondent argued that employers often complain about shortcomings in graduates' ability to work with other people and their ability to communicate confidently, which again may point to the advantages of middle-class social capital:

> communication skills are closely related to confidence. And you know what business is looking for in new graduates; people who can stand up confidently and explain things. Who can put an idea across in a meeting, make an effective presentation. . . . Often a new graduate may be perfectly capable of communicating well orally but if they are not confident with a group of senior people and they are scared of making a fool of themselves, [then] they don't appear to be competent even though they might actually be. It's a vicious circle: low communication skills reduce confidence; low confidence reduces communication skills.

Developing Graduate Employability in University Teaching

Participants were asked to reflect on the ways in which universities might work more closely with employers to develop graduate employability as part of students' university education. The importance of access to the sort of work experience which enables connections to valuable networks and contacts was highlighted by research participants. A senior careers adviser highlighted the importance of paid work experience opportunities and suggested that these might be a compulsory element of undergraduate study:

> Students need to experience working in a workplace environment, using their skills to provide a service that someone is paying for, to truly develop authentic employability skills. We need to offer opportunities for paid work either in a part time capacity or as an internship.

> My personal view is that to enhance employability, all courses should now have a compulsory work experience element(s) throughout the course. Some students are nearing the end of their degree and have never worked and so

from their perspective the transition [into employment] is very difficult and from an employer's perspective they would be getting students who in some cases do not even know what to wear in an office environment.

In terms of the implications for teaching, another careers adviser respondent suggested:

each module and assignment should be linked to how this would be useful in a workplace, with employability threaded throughout. In this way this to some extent circumvents discrepancies in social capital.

Engaging employers in curriculum design and in forging close links with university careers services were thought to be good approaches which contribute to the development of graduate employability. A senior careers adviser, for example, believed that employability should be 'woven into the curriculum', citing employer inputs to curriculum topics, employers offering voluntary or paid placement opportunities and employers contributing to curriculum design and validation processes.

An employability business partner provided some further examples, including a suggestion for some employer involvement in setting assessment:

Within our own institution, employers are becoming increasingly involved in the planning and delivery of some services so they have the chance to shape this too. Other examples include authentic assessment set by employers so students can see what is required from them in a professional context, lecture delivery, real life projects (asking students to use real data to solve problems) and offering experiential opportunities like visits, internships and placements.

Arguably, however, this and some of the other suggestions, such as, for example, learning what to wear in an office environment, may contribute to conceptions of the purposes of higher education as 'training grounds for employment' (Norton, 2016: 155) and acculturation into the norms and expectations of the workplace.

Finding different ways for universities and business to work together was seen as important by our respondents. 'Redesign of the boundary' between university and industry such that the boundary between academia and employers becomes more permeable, with bidirectional benefits and expertise, was one idea for reconceptualizing joint working. The senior academic and business consultant respondent who suggested this also highlighted some of the implications for university teaching:

> One of the things that makes me think that university teaching has to alter, to some degree, is that there needs to be much better integration between university and business. If we could somehow think differently about the way in which universities and business go together it will be one of those real fundamentals that would make us enormously better off. I've worked on this integration as a visiting professor here and in some American universities. In one university, for example, we linked up with a major telecom company and we brought the university in to work on a joint project to upgrade the capability of their technical staff. And the staff got an MSc out of it.

The idea of 'redesigning the boundaries' prompts a different way of thinking about the development of relationships with employers which, as our respondent suggested, has benefits which go both ways – benefits for universities and for businesses. There could be symmetry and mutual benefit in a relationship with business where, for example, students gain opportunities for work placements and internships and in turn business benefits from expertise which academic staff offer, adding value to the business and contributing to professional development of the workforce.

Participants also reflected on some of the challenges they sometimes faced in engaging students in extra-curricular activities, which participants saw as important opportunities to develop their employability. However, a number of issues should be noted which have a bearing on this. For example, not all universities offer these to the same extent, and not all students are in a position to access these equally when factors, including affordability and constraints on students' time, are taken into account. The question of how to engage students with opportunities for work placement experience and careers' services support, and whose responsibility this is, has importance for students and also for universities when judged, among other metrics, on employment outcome measures. Yorke (2004a) put forward that 'The development of employability is a shared responsibility, with institutions, students and employers to the fore' (p. 424). Yet, our respondents suggested that not all students are engaging with the various forms of support and preparation which may help them to gain a work placement. For example, a placement adviser told us:

> Our data from this academic year shows that on the whole students who have engaged on a regular basis with the timetabled sessions have secured

a placement, and those who haven't engaged regularly generally have not secured a placement.

Implications of the Employability Agenda for University Teaching and Teaching Excellence

The foregoing examples suggest that embedding opportunities for work-related learning, placements and skills development for 'career readiness' into the curriculum in order to support graduates' prospects of future entry to the labour market is regarded as desirable within undergraduate programmes. Lowden et al.'s (2011: 25) research recommended: 'One of the most crucial measures HEIs can adopt to promote employability is the provision of integrated placements, internships and work-based learning opportunities of significant duration.' As reported, our respondents favoured threading work experience through the undergraduate curriculum, with one respondent suggesting that every course should include a compulsory element of work experience, which, as they explained, may also help circumvent discrepancies in social capital.

As Saunders and Zuzel (2010: 1) noted, 'One of the key reasons why many students invest in university education is to improve their employment prospects', and periods of work placement and work-based learning may contribute to this. Furthermore, acculturation into the work environment is another consideration (Yorke, 2004a: 423), noted in our study, too. As discussed previously, higher education represents a very significant financial investment and graduate employment and career prospects may be seen as the return on this:

> With the rise in tuition fees, students are investing in their future careers and are more focussed on how the institution can support them to enhance their immediate employment prospects and longer term employability. (Advance HE, 2016)

This suggests that the benefits of higher education are primarily to be seen as private in terms of accruing to individual students. Referring to 'the "public good" nature of education' and the challenges to this which neoliberal economic policy imperatives present, Tilak (2008) pointed to apparent issues of fairness and equity when it comes to accessing opportunities to develop employability and enjoyment of the same benefits. Apposite to this argument about fairness and equity is a trend, noted by Brown, Lauder and Ashton (2012: 9), for corporations to 'gravitate toward global elite universities because they are believed to have the best and brightest students. This focus on attracting, retaining, and developing top talent leads to greater inequality of treatment, as companies seek to identify a cadre of high flyers across the globe.'

While work placement or paid work experience opportunities and internships appear to contribute to students' employability, there are also some important resource implications for universities in locating graduate-level work placement opportunities. The non-elite universities may be particularly disadvantaged in finding high-quality work placement opportunities for students due to resources and networks and sometimes due to the location of the institution. Also, some students may be less able to take advantage of those opportunities, especially if they are unpaid. We conclude this section by identifying some of the implications of the development of undergraduate students' employability for university teaching and teaching excellence.

Employment outcomes are part of the metrics of measuring teaching excellence in higher education in the TEF in the UK context. One problem is that these may be affected by the degree subjects studied. Science, Technology, Engineering and Mathematics (STEM) degree subjects from elite universities, for example, tend to have much better employability outcomes compared with some humanities and social science degree courses at middle-ranked institutions. In addition, graduates from elite universities may also benefit from additional social capital advantages. Kupfer suggests (2011: 204) that 'graduates from the elite universities seem to have a triple advantage: the reputation of the university, social capital networks, and personal or identity capital'.

There are implications for higher education teaching and course design. Yorke (2004a: 410) suggested that 'The adoption of employability as an educational aim necessitates a reconsideration of curriculum design and/or implementation.' Norton (2016) pointed to some of the consequences for curricula design of the push for employability, with a focus on graduate skills and an emphasis on pedagogies such as work-based learning, problem-based learning and skills acquisition prioritized over 'more liberal-inspired values such as knowledge, wisdom and criticality' (p. 155). Some subjects might lend themselves more readily to work-relevant skills and to direct application to work settings than others. A view of teaching excellence limited to the employability skills looked for by employers is arguably a narrow and incomplete idea of the aims and purposes of higher education.

The market logic into which universities and higher education systems are tied (McCowan, 2015) is impacting on changing ideas about what universities are for and their role. Linking graduate employment outcomes to the quality of teaching in universities appears ill-judged not least because, as we have argued, embedding employability in the curriculum does not create employment for graduates. There is a host of other external factors upon which graduate employment depends (McCowan, 2015). In relation to the link in the TEF metrics between graduate employment and teaching excellence, Ashwin (2019) has suggested that this presents a simplified idea of the educational process and distorts how the nature of high-quality university teaching is understood. This link appears to be narrowing the idea of teaching excellence in higher education, for example, equating it to 'work readiness', and risks overlooking what is 'higher' about higher education, while also downplaying wider learning benefits identified by Knight and Yorke (2004). Ashwin (2019) pointed to the role of knowledge and the ways in which the development of a systematic sense of a collective body of knowledge changes how undergraduates think: 'This is a process that is so much more than the development of generic skills. It is a process that fundamentally changes who students are and what they can achieve in the world. It is this process which makes university education a *higher* education.'

From employers' perspectives, there may be an argument for embedding employability within the curriculum and in the extra-curricular non-academic opportunities, too. However, this may be more 'embeddable' within some subjects than others, and a focus on generic skills may sideline the role of academic knowledge. The issue of whether teaching excellence is to be thought of as a process of making students 'work ready' for the labour market is debatable and linked to the purpose of higher education which, as Norton (2016: 155) noted, 'is constantly shifting'. Furthermore, if one of the purposes is acculturation into the world of work, this may include a narrow idea of employability within it.

If subjects that are perceived to offer better prospects of routes into employment are prioritized over non-vocational subjects, then some loss of the social benefits of learning may result, with consequences for the future, as Carasso and Locke (2016: 34) have argued: 'non-vocational subjects are likely to yield higher non-market private and social benefits, such as creativity, intercultural understanding, the development of democratic institutions and the rule of law. The devaluing of these benefits is leading to a long-term skills and knowledge deficit which, in turn, will lead to reductions in overall economic efficiency.'

Conclusion

Tied to the market logic, universities are under pressure in terms of recruitment and student satisfaction scores, and expectations of employment in graduate jobs. Employers also expect employability skills to be developed within the undergraduate curriculum. This chapter has questioned the emphasis on 'work readiness', the role of skills training and the place of this within higher education. A number of key questions about an assumed correspondence between teaching excellence and employment outcomes of graduates in the labour market have been raised in this chapter. How fair and reasonable it is to judge the quality of teaching on external labour market factors has been identified as an issue. Also, the chapter has considered how students' employment outcomes may be enhanced through the social capital advantages enjoyed by some and which may afford access to prestigious and advantageous internships and work placement opportunities which are not all equally available to all students. These may be an important influence on employment outcomes to be considered when attempting to judge the quality of teaching by employment metrics.

The discussion of employers' perspectives on graduate employability and the quality of university undergraduate education in this chapter feeds into the overall argument of the book for an inclusive debate with higher education stakeholder groups about the quality of teaching, teaching excellence and the purposes of higher education. This is examined further in the final chapter.

Points for Discussion

- To what extent should university teaching excellence be judged by graduate employment outcome measures?
- Who should take the main responsibility for the development of students' employability while they are at university?
- What issues are raised when employment metrics are used as proxies for teaching excellence?
- What would be the benefits for employers to be involved in the co-design of university degree curricula?

6

Parents' Perspectives on Teaching Excellence

This chapter examines the idea of teaching excellence from the point of view of parents and its implications for higher education. It draws on previous research (Wood and Su, 2019) undertaken into parents' perspectives of teaching excellence in higher education in England and considers the concept of parents as higher education 'stakeholders'.

This chapter explores the role of parents in students' university decision-making and the value of understanding parents' expectations of university teaching quality. If choices are informed by perceptions of teaching excellence and if parents as stakeholders exert an influence on this, then it is worthwhile to develop understandings of parents' perspectives. We begin by sketching out some background to the policy context and this is followed by an examination of parents as a stakeholder group. Presentation and discussion of the findings of a small-scale study of parents' views of teaching excellence form the central part of the chapter and the potential benefits of continued dialogue with parents during students' undergraduate studies are explored.

Our use of the term 'parents' refers to both parents and carers. At the start of this chapter, there are some particular points to make about the terminology employed when referring to our own research study. First, we recognize that many people are brought up by adults other than their parents. We have opted to use the word 'parents' inclusively to refer to parents and carers, as 'parents' is considered to be a less cumbersome term than 'parents/carers'. Therefore in our usage, 'parents' includes parents and carers. Second, although university students are young adults, we have referred to them as 'children' rather than 'sons/ daughters' or 'young people'. This is more authentic as our parent respondents referred to their own 'children' rather than to 'young people', 'young adults', 'offspring' or other such terms, and some had sons or daughters who were about to go to university and therefore still of school age. Third, we realize that some university students may be in a parental role themselves and that this may add further complexity to the use of the term 'parent'. However, in this chapter we refer to students who are parented rather than students who may themselves be acting in a parenting role.

Context for Parents' Involvement in Higher Education

Embarking on higher education study, having reached the age of eighteen, young adults are continuing their journey towards independence and for which typically their final years of compulsory education would have been preparing them. This chapter considers the support provided by parents that must be seen against the backdrop of a number of factors, which include the higher education funding regime; the ongoing support and involvement of parents during the period of 'emerging adulthood' (Arnett, 2015); and issues of student well-being. The marketization of higher education has been a feature of higher education internationally, driven by neoliberal imperatives (Gourlay and Stevenson, 2017: 391). In a system of higher education which is governed by principles of competition and marketization, informed consumer choice is regarded as a mechanism to raise the standards of teaching. For instance, in the UK context, these intentions were clear when the TEF was introduced in 2016: 'this Government will introduce a Teaching Excellence Framework (TEF), to provide clear information to students about where the best provision can be found and to drive up the standard of teaching in all universities' (Department for Business, Innovation and Skills, 2016: 13 para. 26).

The market is intended to act as a mechanism for incentivizing universities to 'raise their game' (Department for Business, Innovation and Skills, 2016: 8 para. 7). Within this system the student, positioned as a customer, is envisaged to benefit from increased competition across the sector: 'By introducing more competition and informed choice into higher education, we will deliver better outcomes and value' (Department for Business, Innovation and Skills 2016: 8 para. 6). In such a business environment, the term 'stakeholders' does not seem out of place. Understood as 'any group or individual who can affect or is affected by the achievement of the firm's objectives', the role of stakeholders is 'vital' to business success (Freeman, 2010: 25). In the role of 'customers', students and their parents have a financial stake in higher education as 'the shift from state to individual responsibility has in practice been a shift to both individuals *and* families wherever parents are willing and able to offer financial support' (Lewis and West, 2017: 1251).

'Informed choice' is a key term in the policy discourse: 'For competition in the HE sector to deliver the best possible outcomes, students must be able to make informed choices' (Department for Business, Innovation and Skills, 2016: 11 para. 18) and the TEF metrics are intended as a source of information about teaching quality, as 'The TEF will provide clear, understandable information to students about where teaching quality is outstanding' (Department for Business, Innovation and Skills, 2016: 13 para. 26).

Global, regional and national rankings of universities are produced and published in the media, and 'students and their parents remain the primary audience for rankings' (Hazelkorn, 2015: xiv). In terms of the UK and the TEF awards, while the TEF assessment outcome is not supposed to be a ranking (Brink, 2018,: 136), it can be seen as such: for 'Every 'provider' with a gold award clearly outranks everyone with a silver award, and likewise silver outranks bronze' (Brink, 2018: 136). Parents are influential sources of information for students in their choice of university (Johnston, 2010). Brooks (2004: 495) noted that evidence from large-scale surveys shows that when young people are thinking about their higher education choices, 'parents are the most commonly consulted group of people'. Lewis and West's (2017) research found that parents were more likely to be providing financial support for their children through the university years and beyond (p. 1260). Similarly, Heath and Calvert (2013: 1121) refer to continued dependence on family support as 'a common feature of the lives of many young adults, colouring their experiences of independent living'. Given the higher education landscape and the pressures of marketization, it may be timely for universities to rethink the ways in which they engage parents in developing understandings of teaching quality and how excellence is judged and evidenced. The next section considers the positioning of parents as higher education stakeholders.

Parents as a 'Stakeholder' Group in Higher Education

The reader may question why parents are considered to be 'stakeholders' at all when on reaching the post-compulsory stage of education at the age of eighteen, young people are deemed to have entered adulthood. It could be argued that having left the compulsory phase of education, the relationship of parents to university is very different from the previous parental role and relationship with the school, which acted in loco parentis. However, funding policy in higher education in England assumes parental contribution in terms of financial support and 'an inextricable link continues to be made between students and their families with regard to the funding regime' (West et al., 2015: 25).

In England, student tuition fees are financed through tuition loans. Students accumulate annual tuition debt to be repaid when income earned reaches a certain threshold level (Marginson, 2018). For many students, university choice is made while in the final year of school. In the White Paper 'Success as a Knowledge Economy: Teaching Excellence, Social Mobility and Student Choice', young people and their parents are assumed to be involved in the decision-making: 'it is vital that young people and their parents have access to the best possible information to help them make the right choices' (Department for Business, Innovation and Skills, 2016: 57).

Transition into adulthood today can be protracted. More young adults live with their parents than a decade earlier (The Intergenerational Commission, 2018). 'Emerging adulthood' (Arnett, 2015: 8) is a term used to refer to 'longer and more widespread education, later entry to marriage and parenthood, and a prolonged and erratic transition to stable work'. Debt, poor growth in earnings and a significant proportion of income spent on housing costs contribute to increased dependence on family support (Heath and Calvert, 2013; The Intergenerational Commission, 2018). Parents' involvement in decision-making regarding university choice and their financial contribution to higher education in the prevailing funding system may suggest that they can be considered as a stakeholder group having a 'vested interest'. Their 'stake' in higher education perhaps needs to be viewed in this context and 'most emerging adults want and need their parents' support into their twenties. The emerging adults who struggle the most are not the ones suffering from the invasion of helicopter parents, but the ones who cannot count on their parents' love and support even when they need them' (Arnett, 2015: 67). The term 'emerging adulthood' refers to a 'life stage', an 'in-between period', between adolescence and young adulthood (Arnett, 2015).

While Arnett's frame of reference is society in the United States, the demographic changes that define emerging adulthood are an international phenomenon (Arnett, 2015: 8). Today's parents may be considered as a group having 'paid in' to higher education and, therefore, to have a financial stake. The prolonged involvement of parents is to be viewed against the backdrop of the direction of policy change from the public to the private, from state responsibility to individual responsibility. This has, as we noted earlier drawing on the work of Lewis and West (2017), relocated responsibility for the costs of higher education, shifting it to individual students and to parents who are willing and have the means to provide financial support. Lewis and West (2017: 1251) also observe that 'Similarly, housing costs and the effects of the recession on graduate employment have prolonged graduates' dependence on parents, again where they are willing and able.' Some groups of students may have reasons to choose an institution near to home when deciding where to study: 'Geographical distance between parental home and college poses a potential barrier to higher education entry, and could be a deciding factor when choosing between institutions. Low income and ethnic minority groups are often considered to be especially constrained in their education choices because they need to stay at home for financial or cultural reasons,' Gibbons and Vignoles (2012: 98) maintained in a study of these issues in England.

However, 'involvement' may assume different forms, ranging from peripheral to centre-stage and is not necessarily assumed to be a benign idea. Some of the possible ramifications of excessive parental involvement are considered in the literature in relation to 'helicoptering' parenting styles. Helicoptering was alluded to previously in the quote from Arnett (2015); originating in the United States, the term 'helicopter parents' is used to refer to 'those who closely monitor their student offspring and who are ready to intervene at any sign of difficulty' (Lewis et al., 2015: 417). Von Bergen and Bressler (2017: 3) use the term to refer to 'excessive levels of involvement, advice, problem-solving, control, protection, and abundant and unnecessary tangible assistance in the service of their offspring's well-being'.

Drawing on higher education in a North American context, Von Bergen and Bressler's (2017: 4) examples of 'helicopter' parenting of their college-aged adult children amount to this excessive 'hovering' and over-protection. This, it could be argued, may present an obstacle to the development of independent judgement:

> Critical thinking was once understood to be the mark of a person who had been in receipt of a higher education. Indeed, there was considerable overlap between the liberal conception of the idea of the university and the idea of critical thinking. The university precisely made available a space in which the mind could be so educated that it was able to form its own authentic judgments. (Davies and Barnett, 2015: 2)

Overzealous 'helicoptering' by parents may be an impediment when it comes to opportunities for young adults to learn how to problem-solve and to assume responsibility for their lives (Von Bergen and Bressler, 2017).

The idea of teaching excellence is situated within the wider discourse on the purposes of higher education (Runté and Runté, 2018: 66). When considering the aims and purpose of higher education over half a century ago, the Robbins Report (1963) conceptualized the 'essence' of higher education as introducing students 'to a world of intellectual responsibility and intellectual discovery in which they are to play their part' (para 555). A capacity for critical thought may be considered intrinsic to the aims and purposes of higher education. It could be argued that increased engagement of parents may curtail student agency and their experience of higher education as induction into the 'world of intellectual responsibility and intellectual discovery' and the development of independent critical thought. However, the particular needs of some students, for example, vulnerable young people within the student population, are relevant to this discussion of the role of parents. Tressler and Piper (2017) note that

> For students, the uniqueness of living in an environment with hundreds of young people for the first time is a major life transition. Many issues present themselves at this time of change: homesickness, living with strangers and making friends, problems with the integration between home and university care, drugs and alcohol, security and safety, and managing the lack of a pastoral support system.

This raises some critical and significant issues relevant to discussions of extended emergence into adulthood, the role of parents and responsibility for student well-being. Engagement with parents may be beneficial in supporting students' well-being as they transition to university. Dialogue and engagement with parents may also be useful to develop understandings of parents' perceptions of the wider aims and purposes of higher education, teaching quality and excellence. This suggests a role for the development of channels for communication and some forms of dialogue with parents. This may well present challenges, not least because of the complexities of engaging a heterogeneous group with a range of assumptions and beliefs in such an interchange (see Bohm, 2004).

Parents' Perspectives on Teaching Excellence

Situating teaching excellence within a wider narrative of the purposes of higher education adds to understandings of the political drivers and some of the problems inherent in a narrow focus on 'teaching excellence'. As Collini (2012: 198) notes, the teaching role 'is certainly central to most universities, but it is far from being the whole story'. He refers to their important role in 'conserving, understanding, extending, and handing on to subsequent generations the intellectual, scientific, and artistic heritage of mankind' (p.198). Focusing on the teaching role and the TEF may mean that wider aspects of what universities do and contribute are insufficiently recognized. Dialogue with parents may help to counter reductivist and instrumental understandings of the value of higher education and what universities do and contribute to the intellectual life of the nation, by setting discussion of teaching excellence within a wider framework of understanding: 'Major universities are complex organisms, fostering an extraordinary variety of intellectual, scientific and cultural activity, and the significance and value of much that goes on within them cannot be restricted to a single national framework or to the present generation' (Collini, 2012: 198).

Marketization has been a feature of neoliberal policies in higher education. Brink (2018: 140) notes the association between the TEF and student fees: 'from the outset, it was linked to the contentious issue of student fees. The idea was that a university which does well enough in its TEF rating would thereby earn the right to raise their student fees.' He identifies the presupposition behind this, namely that 'Higher education is, or should be treated as, a market economy, which in turn is based on the conception that a university education is essentially a private benefit. The student will benefit, so the student should bear the cost, but should also have consumer rights, such as relating price to quality' (Brink, 2018: 140). Given that higher education funding policy assumes a parental financial contribution, and therefore parents may well be part-bearers of the costs, parents' views of teaching excellence have importance. Peters (2004: 71) suggests that 'in the age of global capitalism universities have been reduced to a technical ideal of performance within a contemporary discourse of "excellence"'. Engaging parents in dialogue may 'augment understanding' of how excellence is framed within neoliberal policy discourse and the contentious issue of portraying the many-layered concept of teaching excellence through metrics and rankings. Given changes to the funding of higher education in England, which impact on parents and the role of parents in young people's decision-making in choice of university, these are significant issues affecting them and their children. Lewis and West (2017) observed that 'in England, both the introduction of student loans to cover the costs of higher education, and changes in the structure of the housing and labour markets has had an impact on families', and they refer to the 'great risk shift away', that is, from public to private, state to family, in line with neoliberal ideas (p. 1251). Forrester and Garratt (2016: 9) refer to the 1980s and 1990s as years marked by a 'shift away from the social-democratic consensus towards neo-liberalism and the market as the main source of resource distribution'. In higher education policy, 'the market has been substituted for the state: students are now "customers" or "clients" and teachers are "providers"' (Peters, 2004: 73).

The foregoing discussion of the stakeholder concept, ideological perspectives and the policy environment provides some background relevant to the development of understandings of parents' perspectives on teaching excellence in higher education. It is to this that we now turn our attention, and we draw on data from our own small-scale qualitative research study of parents' perspectives on teaching excellence (Wood and Su, 2019).[1] To protect anonymity, respondents were coded numerically (for example, the designation 'R1' refers to respondent 1). Often 'respondent' is used in full but occasionally 'R' is used as an abbreviation, followed by the appropriate number.

There was a concern expressed by our research respondents, as customers, to see a return on their 'investment'. The university's role in preparing their children for future careers was important to them, and our data suggested that a university education was seen as a significant investment for the students and their families, both emotionally and financially. Some respondents indicated that they maintained a close involvement with their children's university experience and offered emotional support as needed in the case of any personal struggles with university life.

While emphasizing expectations of better career prospects as an outcome of gaining a degree, parents also recognized the limitations of narrow conceptions of the value and purposes of higher education when seen simply in terms of 'usefulness' or through simple metrics and quality indicators of 'value for money'. It was interesting that while parents' expectations of teaching excellence appeared to be influenced by a neoliberal policy context, their views of the wider and less tangible purposes of higher education ran alongside it. As Respondent 6 who had one child still at school suggested:

> I have a strong belief that higher education is an end in itself – that studying for a degree is valuable because it allows you to think, explore, broaden your horizons, develop 'soft' skills such as critical thinking, teamwork, how to be independent. It exposes you to ideas and perspectives you may not have experienced before.

Another respondent (R21), with a child studying at university, also pointed to the learning experience and wider benefits of university education:

> I agree with what people have said about universities being a wonderful place of formation as well as a place of learning. What I also sort of see as a very different kind of learning experience than you get from secondary school. My hope is that my daughter will gain that love of intellectual curiosity and so I think the idea of independent intellectual pursuit, which university does encourage. For me, it's also about social skills, the whole formation of yourself as an independent young adult.

These remarks from the respondents seem to suggest that the value of university education cannot be fully appreciated by metrics, such as the TEF metrics. The participating parents appear to afford value to a range of benefits from higher education and perhaps with echoes of Robbins' (1963) idea, referred to earlier in the chapter, of higher education as an introduction 'to a world of intellectual responsibility and intellectual discovery in which they are to play their part' (para. 555). The words 'in which they are to play their part' seems apt today, implying the active part played by the learner and a contrast to consumerism and higher education as a commodity.

Conceptions of Teaching Excellence

Many respondents reported that they expected academics to be experts in the subject taught, to be passionate about their subject, and able to excite and engage students. For example, Respondent 17, who had two children studying at school, saw this passion for the subject as part of what teaching excellence was about, together with the pedagogic knowledge and expertise to use a variety of teaching and learning strategies.

> For me, teaching excellence would be about people who are passionate about their subject and who can excite and engage my son. So, I think that teaching excellence is both about, you know, kind of how you present it, the activities that you do, you know, whether you use kind of lectures too much. It's about having a balance of different ways of teaching and that's kind of the technical side of it. But alongside that somebody's personality is also important.

In respondents' remarks, there was an emphasis on academics' ability to communicate, their technical 'know-how' when it comes to their pedagogic capability as evident in the diversity of their teaching styles, and their personality and enthusiasm. It is important to be wary of emphasizing any one particular aspect and, as Gregory (2013) reminds us: 'Teaching excellence can never be reduced to the operation of a single variable, no matter how attractive that variable might be.' He argues that 'teaching excellence can be thought about systematically as an intellectual and ethical project, not just emotive performance' (p.140). While enthusiasm, passion and teaching ability factored into parents' perceptions of teaching excellence, they also recognized other variables such as pedagogy, effective communication and, as we will come on to next, attention to individual needs and knowing how to connect with and engage students.

For some respondents, their children's relations with academics were seen as a key element of teaching excellence, believing teaching excellence to be evident when academics recognize an individual student's needs and support him/her accordingly. This would require academics' attentiveness, differentiation and a focus on individual potential in their teaching practice. Respondent 1, who had a child currently at university, seemed to capture 'teaching excellence' in terms of the relevance of 'what' is studied and also 'how' the lecturer 'delivers' this, and pointed to the importance of staff being passionate about their subject and of caring about the students they teach. Respondent R19, with two children studying at school, considered that excellent teachers develop a close knowledge of their students.

> Excellent teachers pay attention to each individual student. The teacher knows each of the students very well, psychologically or what deep-down kind of person this young person will develop into. So that the teacher will find out a way to motivate this person.

Parents gave priority to teaching that develops students' confidence and which 'draws students out of themselves', as suggested by Respondent R18 who had one child studying at university.

> It is about two-way conversation because we know at 18 unless they are very confident they tend to just sit and not put their head above the parapet. Where for me, teaching excellence is about to draw students out of themselves and to start having the conversations and to be seen that, yeah, the tutor has the subject knowledge but equally their input can contribute to that and together they're on a learning journey.

Parents also related teaching excellence to teaching that, among other things, develops critical thinking, as suggested in the following comments from Respondent 13 who had one child studying at university.

> Excellent teaching inspires, challenges, develops critical thinking and leaves students with a love of their subject and a clear sense of their strengths and areas to improve on.

The parents' responses appeared to point to a pedagogy based on dialogue and to the development of learners' self-confidence and critical thinking as features of excellent teaching. There were echoes of this in previous comments too, for example, the idea that 'studying for a degree is valuable because it allows you to think, explore, broaden your horizons'. Excellent teaching was considered to support student preparation for the future, for example, through 'the whole formation of yourself as an independent young adult'. To some respondents, excellence was evidenced in a teacher's ability to appreciate the challenges that learners may experience and an emphasis on talking to students and helping them when learning proves difficult. For example, Respondent 18 with one child studying at university, expressed her thoughts:

> I think, as well, it's about that relationship within the classroom and it's also about the teacher exposing themselves, so to speak, by saying, well, I've been where you are and I found that really difficult. But if we try and talk about what it is, try and explore what you're struggling with.

Here the respondent appeared to point to empathy as a necessary quality which academics need to develop in their teaching practice. If academics admitted to having experienced such challenges themselves, then parents considered that this could act as a powerful incentive to strengthen students' resolve to face these challenges and overcome them. Again, this reflects the idea of what Gregory (2013: 201) referred to as 'teacherly ethos': 'Teacherly ethos is not so much about what a teacher should *do* (in an instrumental or methodological sense) as about who a teacher should *be* (in terms of character and virtue). Students care little about what methods their teachers use but do care immensely about what kinds of persons their teachers are.' Our respondent suggested that excellent teaching may include teachers exposing their own struggles with the subject and in this way giving an insight into themselves as people and experiences they have in common with their students.

Seeing an integral link between teaching and learning, some respondents cautioned against discussing teaching excellence in a vacuum, without also referring to the students and their learning, as Respondent 17, with two children studying at school, suggested.

> I think it's really difficult to talk about teaching without talking about learning and I think things that we've been saying, you know, you want the tutor or the teacher to know the student, you want them to understand how they learn best and I think, you know, there is a danger today that we talk about teaching excellence and the focus is on the tutor and the teaching and it's not on the learners and, of course, a good teacher understands that.

Along similar lines, some respondents highlighted the importance of the role and responsibility of the learner in teaching excellence. For example, Respondent 24, with two children having completed university and one currently studying at university, considered that:

> It's about the individual students and how committed they are to learning . . . as well as the standard of the university.

Another respondent (R20, with one child having completed university and one child currently studying at university) appeared to share this understanding of the learner's part:

> It is down to the young adult themselves. So, we could be in an excellent university and next daughter could be at a poor university but the one in the

poor university could really excel because they've got drive, determination of their own.

These comments suggest a perceived need for a concept of teaching excellence to include the roles of teacher and learner in it. In the current discourse of teaching excellence, there is an overemphasis on responsibility of academics and it appears the parents were very clear that to achieve the desirable learning outcomes, there is an equal responsibility on the part of learners.

Measurability and Indicators of Teaching Excellence

When asked about the measurability of teaching excellence, many respondents expressed the view that teaching excellence should be measured or judged, and various indicators were suggested. While favouring measurement of some aspects of teaching excellence, they also recognized that the 'essence' of teaching excellence may be impossible to capture in simple metrics, and this seemed to be where they recognized that judgement plays a part. The idea that judgement is involved may suggest a more nuanced understanding. Respondent 10, with one child currently at university and another one at school, shared her thoughts on forms of evidence:

> I think teaching excellence is about both the quality of lectures, but also the quality of seminars and tutorials. It is also about being available for students who may have questions. It should be measured by observation, auditing marking, availability of lecture notes, speed of marking, and the attitude of lecturers, i.e. showing a commitment to teaching over research.

Another respondent (R6), with one child at school, appeared to suggest some quantitative and qualitative indicators and measures:

> I think 'teaching excellence' relates to a number of indicators (e.g. contact hours, employability etc.). I would like it to relate more to outcomes (has the student made the progress expected?), and student voice, and perhaps through qualitative measures (e.g. observation, work scrutiny).

At the same time, some parents raised concerns with measuring teaching excellence, and parent respondent R13, with one child having recently completed university study and another one currently at university, appeared to recognize that there are difficulties in measuring excellence in ways that really capture its 'essence':

> I'm not sure it can be measured in a way that gets to the essence, but it should not be measured by simple metrics and/or data just because it can be easily collected. The views of teachers and students of the experience and their reflections on it are part of the evidence but not in ways that reduce evidence collection to simple surveys of whether the teaching was enjoyable or not.

Graduate employability as an indicator of teaching excellence was perceived to be problematic by some parents. For example, Respondent 21, who had one child studying at university, shared her thoughts:

> I think that one of the ideas to judge on employability at the end, I think, is terribly problematic. I think it's problematic if you're in Humanities degree, it depends on what kind of degree you're doing. I also think it's problematic because people get jobs for all sorts of reasons and people with advantages get jobs because they know people and people who don't have those advantages might not get those jobs so I think it's a really, really problematic thing, to just draw an equal sign between degree and employability.

This respondent appeared to allude to the idea of social capital and the advantages it can bring. 'The central idea of social capital is that social networks are a valuable asset' (Field, 2017: 2), and this respondent referred to people with advantages getting jobs 'because they know people'. However, 'Social capital can promote inequality because access to networks is itself unequally distributed. Everyone can use their connections as a way of advancing their interests, but some people's connections are more valuable than that of others' (Field, 2017: 50), an idea apparently echoed in the respondent's subsequent comment that 'people who don't have those advantages might not get those jobs'.

Respondents indicated a recognition of aspects of teaching excellence that they felt could be evidenced and quantified and also an acknowledgement that some aspects defy measurement. This could include, for example, the 'feel' of the institution, openness, the passion conveyed by academics for the subjects taught and whether the institution cares about and supports students' learning needs: 'Once we begin to measure, we begin to tick boxes and then we always, always lose something,' one respondent told us. Their conceptions of how teaching excellence is to be measured and judged therefore could be seen to range from very specific expectations expressed in performance measures, including contact hours, attendance, programme completion, student feedback and student satisfaction data, research quality, degree results and employability after university, to judgements of the more intuitive and affective aspects of teaching and learning. It was suggested that the latter should not be overlooked in favour of simple metrics which can be more easily collected and are more amenable to measurement.

Implications

Whether it is appropriate to consider parents as a 'stakeholder' group in higher education at all has been the subject of some scrutiny in this chapter. We have suggested that a rigid distinction between school pupil and university student is, in reality, somewhat blurred. For example, the ethos and practice in the sixth form is different from that in the eleven to sixteen years age range, and a rigid divide which sees students as independent and self-directed adults on entering higher education would be a facile assumption. Therefore a continuing need on the part of students as young adults for help and support in journeying towards becoming independent, self-directed autonomous beings may be closer to the mark, and we have suggested and presented reasons to support an argument for parents to have a continued role in this. The very idea that at some point we become independent, self-directed and self-motivated learners, once and for all, may itself be contentious and questionable.

We have examined what parents hope will be gained by their children from a university education, and their views of teaching excellence appeared to be influenced by their expectations of higher education and what they saw as its purposes. Parents appeared to see the economic benefits in terms of enhanced career prospects and earnings as one of the purposes of a degree to some extent, but while also hoping that higher education would broaden a young person's outlook and enable him/her to gain a more expansive view of the world. The latter they expressed in terms of the value of higher education as 'an end in itself', representing an opportunity to 'think, explore and broaden your horizons', inculcating a 'love of intellectual curiosity' and contributing to 'the formation of independent young adults'. These two views are not incompatible. However, the expectation of enhanced employment prospects may pose a problem for universities, for example, if there is a lack of graduate jobs. Brink (2018: 216) has suggested that 'The reason why parents are so anxious for their children to go to a "good school" and then on to a "good university" are essentially utilitarian: it will serve them in having a "good career", which is a euphemism for earning more money.' A question raised by this is, of course, how we define and measure 'good' or 'excellent', a point which is also made by Brink (2018: xvii): 'Behind almost any discussion about universities is the question of quality. What makes a "good university"? This question, which occupies not only academics but millions of parents and prospective students, is of course only a proxy for a more fundamental question: what we mean by "good"?' In his discussion of the UK TEF, Ashwin (2017: 11) has considered the assessment criteria that underpin how excellence is judged within the TEF and suggested that it is unclear 'how they form a coherent whole that tell us something important about the excellence of teaching or what the view of teaching is that underpins them'.

Parents had an expectation of enhanced career prospects and, as Blyth and Cleminson (2016) noted, attaining the necessary skills and qualifications they need to realize their career ambitions is an important motivation for many students entering higher education (p. 8). However, arguably a problem with this expectation, as indicated earlier, is that the employment prospects of graduates are part of a broader picture of the economy. According to a report in the *Financial Times* (O'Connor, 2013): 'Each cohort of graduates since the financial crisis is earning less than the one before.' An economic downturn and a lack of high-skill job opportunities available to graduates, for example, are not of universities' making. Ford (2016: 250) noted that 'The reality is that awarding more university degrees does not increase the fraction of the workforce engaged in the professional, technical, and managerial jobs that most graduates would like to land.' As Barkas et al. (2019: 808) have commented:

> It is not clear whether employability is a generic outcome of the 'right' university education, i.e. an 'institutional achievement', or 'the propensity of the individual student to get employment' (Harvey 2001, 97). Indeed, the individual-level teaching excellence of academics may be a capability that enhances graduates' employability.
>
> In some senses, therefore, the linkage between the TEF and employability is not, in fact, as direct as policy-makers in the relevant government department (s) may think.

Arguably, therefore, the metrics currently used to measure teaching excellence are not necessarily adequate to address parents' expectations and concerns about university teaching quality, as discussed earlier in the chapter.

Conclusion

In conclusion, parents' perceptions of teaching excellence as a higher education stakeholder group appear to raise some important implications for higher education institutions. Maintaining a continued dialogue in some form with parents may have benefits for students' experience of continuity of support and may help in their transition to adulthood. There may be benefits for universities, too, in establishing a dialogue with parents during the period of a student's study at university to share perspectives of teaching excellence and the purposes and wider benefits of higher education. This may help to build understandings and thereby reduce some of the tensions inherent in policy rhetoric and influencing practices in higher education today. We have recognized the complexities and challenges that this may present as well as the potential benefits in building an extended appreciation of roles and informing one another's perspectives on matters of excellence and purpose.

Points for Discussion

- How do parents' perceptions of teaching excellence inform their children's choice of university?
- Is there a place for continued dialogue between universities and parents during their children's university education?
- Given the heterogeneity of parents as a stakeholder group what might be the possible implications for engaging their perspectives?
- How might universities take parents' perspectives into account in developing teaching excellence?

7

Towards an Inclusive Perspective on Teaching Excellence

In this book, we have argued that there is a real need to engage the plurality of stakeholders' perspectives in debates of teaching excellence. Informed public debate has been advocated to examine and reshape prevailing manifestations of teaching excellence, which enact assumptions grounded in a dominant and pervasive market logic. At the outset, and noting that some commentators are now suggesting that we are moving into a post-neoliberal era, the timeliness to revisit and debate teaching excellence provided an important part of the framing for this project. So, too, did the imperative to think about who these debates should be with. Inclusive civic debate has been advocated to stimulate curiosity and to wonder, for example, whether teaching excellence could be thought about in other ways and what it might look like in a new post-liberal dispensation. Against this backdrop, it appears an opportune moment to examine the discourse of teaching excellence and envision a more inclusive debate. The development of inclusive perspectives on teaching excellence must capture the heterogeneity of stakeholder constituencies and find ways to overcome some of the challenges of engaging with multiple and under-represented voices. Inclusive perspectives may be built more meaningfully through relationships and dialogue than reliance on tools such as surveys and students may be overloaded with surveys and with tick box evaluations. Partnership approaches grounded in pedagogical relationships of trust may elicit rich qualitative understandings and create opportunities to engage student voices in shaping the development of excellent teaching. Arguably this is nurtured through a 'community of learning' ethos in the classroom because 'real learning does not happen until students are brought into relationship with the teacher, with each other, and with the subject. We cannot learn deeply and well until a community of learning is created in the classroom' (Palmer, 1993: xvi).

In the first chapter the idea of the moment was invoked: 'The moment is born of the everyday and within the everyday' (Lefebvre, 2014:519). Moments are 'experiences of detachment from the everyday flow of time, or durée' (Chen, 2017:28). According to Lefebvre, 'the moment is not the same as a situation, but it creates them' (Elden, 2004:173). The 'moment' is 'somehow revelatory of the total possibiliies contained in daily existence' (Harvey, 1991:429), and detaching from the dominant quantification, consumerism and market logics that now imbue everyday ways of speaking and thinking about teaching excellence, this book has envisioned other possibilities so that 'what is impossible in the everyday becomes what is possible' (Lefebvre, 2014:516).

Importance of Stakeholders' Perspectives on Teaching Excellence

Influenced by market-led models of operation, we have examined how language and practices from the business world are now commonly adopted by the university sector. Universities craft their 'brand image', carve out their 'market niche' and are aware of the influence of image and rankings on student choice: 'Students have an increasing amount of comparative data available to them, often in the form of rankings that tell them where the greatest prestige is to be gained. Universities work hard to present themselves in the best possible light, selecting carefully from league table positions and other badges of quality' (Blackmore, 2016: 9). In such a competitive environment, universities face many challenges, including a myriad of stakeholders who are 'making more demands, with more access to data that depict quality than ever before' (Blackmore, 2016: 67). As Light, Cox and Calkins (2009: 4) remark, 'Higher education is business.' In the business world, it makes good commercial sense to identify who the stakeholders are and to understand them and respond to their expectations. Higher education is often spoken about in terms which at one time would have seemed out of place in the realm of public service provision. As Light, Cox and Calkins (2009: 4) note, 'This commercial language, drawn from the corporate world, has infiltrated most, if not all, of the features of higher education, sitting uncomfortably alongside older terms it augments or even replaces.' Given that in this environment universities must market themselves to gain advantage over their competitors and operate as efficient business organizations, the importance of knowing who their stakeholder groups are, what they expect, how they judge excellence and the 'product' on offer, may be considered as vital for today's university sector as it is in the world of commerce.

In this book our concern is with teaching excellence, and we contend that to understand stakeholders' expectations these must be set in the context of the prevailing higher education policy environment and the positioning of stakeholder groups within it. Blackmore notes that, encouraged by deliberate government policy in many countries, competitiveness is more apparent than it ever was in the academy (2016: 1). In this competitive market environment, in which stakeholders' choices are seen as a mechanism to drive quality and excellence, our concern is to explore how universities might engage their stakeholder 'publics', democratize debate and build civic understandings of what constitutes teaching excellence and the wider purposes of higher education. This is a significant task in a policy climate which positions and constructs stakeholders in particular ways and when, as noted earlier, 'In all directions the academy is increasingly competitive, and a more traditional rhetoric of collegiality seems threadbare' (Blackmore, 2016: 1). This is the backdrop for the exploration in this chapter of how more meaningful relationships with stakeholders might be cultivated, and this discussion is set in the context of the wider role of the university in civic society.

We have separated out different stakeholder groups rather than referring more generally to 'university stakeholders' because we recognize the distinctiveness of the constituencies within the broad stakeholder community. There are internal and external stakeholders, primary and secondary stakeholders, and subgroups within each of these as well as overlaps, too. These are not discrete groupings either, for it is also possible to be located within more than one stakeholder group.

A call for inclusive understandings of teaching excellence embraces higher education both as a common public good and as an individual private benefit. In this argument for the role of stakeholder perspectives in developing understandings of teaching excellence, individual private benefits may coexist with benefits for society and higher education as a public good: what is commonly good for individual people who collectively form 'the public'. This is captured in Nixon's idea of the public as 'the actuality of people working together for their own and others' good' (2012: 16). Proceeding from this position, possibilities arise for civic engagement of stakeholders in critical public debate about the future of higher education and re-examination of the policy discourse of teaching excellence. However, drawing clear distinctions between 'public' and 'private' is not as straightforward as may be imagined: 'Public and private sometimes compete, sometimes complement each other, and sometimes are merely parts of a larger series of classifications that includes, say, local, domestic, personal, political, economic, or intimate. Almost every major cultural change – from Christianity to printing to psychoanalysis – has left a new sedimentary layer in the meaning of public and private' (Warner, 2002: 28). Higher education now tends to be perceived as a private good. Quality is to be improved through the sum of individual choices, the costs are ultimately borne by individuals and the benefits primarily accrue to individuals – an ideological stance which impoverishes the idea of higher education as a matter of public good. Our understanding of higher education as a public good is informed by Nixon (2012: 1), who defines a public good as 'a good that, being more than the aggregate of individual interests, denotes a common commitment to social justice and equality'. Individualism and the benefits of higher education when seen primarily in private terms are not conducive to a climate of public debate. The grip of the state on the control of higher education in the UK is clear, despite the rhetoric from the central government of 'choice', 'freedoms' and 'flexibility': 'Ministers of state may inform us that the state no longer governs from a single locus of power, but devolves power through networks of governance; yet state control of higher education through admissions and funding policies and through the mechanisms of bureaucratic accountability becomes increasingly invasive' (Nixon, 2012: 15).

The Discourse of 'the Public'

Our project is motivated by a desire to engage public debate about higher education and the discourse of teaching excellence. Such debate is at the heart of democracy and fundamental to the idea of higher education as a matter of the public good: 'The public good is not an abstraction, but the actuality of people working together for their own and others' good' (Nixon, 2012: 16). To refer to 'the stakeholders' of a university as a broad grouping would seem to embrace some of the assumptions explored by Warner (2002: 65), who unpacks the idea of '*the* public' and argues that 'People do not always distinguish even between *the* pubic and *a* public, though in certain contexts the difference can matter a great deal. *The* public is a kind of social totality. Its most common sense is that of people in general'. There are many different groupings – 'publics' – and a totalizing notion of 'the public' may not do justice to the plurality of the public sphere. In discussing *the* public, Warner continues:

> It might be the people organized as the nation, the commonwealth, the city, the state, or some other community. It might be very general, as in Christendom or humanity. But in each case, the public, as a people, is thought to include everyone within the field in question. This sense of totality is brought out by speaking of *the* public, even though to speak of a national public implies that others exist; there must be as many publics as polities, but whenever one is addressed as *the* public, the others are assumed not to matter. (Warner, 2002: 65–6)

The plurality of the public sphere is central to our book. The diversity of stakeholder perspectives is an acknowledgement that diversity exists in the public sphere and the different shades and nuances each brings adds to the development of understandings. We argue that we can still legitimately conceive of a public realm that embraces individual and cultural difference: the notion of 'the public' can embrace difference, diversity and disagreement. In the UK context, how stakeholder groups are defined and legitimized within the current system relates to the current divisive nature of politics within the UK and the perceived need for a party-political system that reflects the diverse and interconnected constituencies that comprise society across all of the UK's countries and regions. The idea of 'the public' implies only one acceptable voice, and this can be linked to the ascendancy of populist discourse. For example, drawing on the UK context, the public debate about the UK's departure from the European Union has been characterized by claims from supporters of 'leave' that their interpretation of what leave means is supported by 'the public' with reference to the 2016 referendum result. However, this position takes no account of the relatively narrow margin of the vote in favour of leaving the

EU (52 per cent to 48 per cent) nor the lack of clarity about the details of the departure and the UK's future relationship with the EU. The reference to 'the public's view' fails to recognize the spectrum of opinion, the diversity of positions and the practical concerns of many different groups (e.g. UK citizens living in the EU, EU citizens resident in the UK, the impact of the UK/Republic of Ireland border on the lives of people in Northern Ireland). The discourse about 'the public' prevents a wider dialogue seeking to build consensus about the meaning of being outside the EU and the opportunity to seek 'losers' consent' for such a profound and long-lasting constitutional change. The discourse of a single public also fosters the conditions which contribute to the growth of a divisive identity politics, in which political loyalties are constructed based on cultural characteristics rather than political ideologies. This kind of politics undermines the party-political system by making it harder to sustain groupings and coalitions of different views. The notion of the broad church, once central to the British political system, is replaced by the narrow sect or cult. Realigning politics on the basis of identity in this way also allows the growth of the view that certain identities have greater legitimacy; as the public voted for Brexit, that is now the dominant and acceptable voice. All other voices and the identities they represent are thus marginalized and even dismissed with the bellicose language of treachery and conflict.

In this chapter we acknowledge the heterogeneity of stakeholders and, in examining different stakeholders' perspectives, the aim is not to arrive at an idealized, bland accord. Nor is the aim to advocate dialogue as a means to build a consensus across stakeholder groups and to airbrush out and delegitimize some voices as 'outliers'. The idea of the plurality of the public sphere is central to our conceptualization of an inclusive perspective. Pluralism is embraced in the way we frame our understanding of 'the public'. When referring to 'dialogue', this is understood in the sense in which Appiah uses the word 'conversation': 'not only for literal talk but also as a metaphor for engagement with the experience and the ideas of others' (Appiah, 2007: 85).

In support of our argument for the development of public participation in constructing understandings of teaching excellence, the perspectives of a number of different stakeholder groups have been drawn on in this book, while also recognizing that within these broad groupings there are finer distinctions that can be made and that the current groupings are inevitably generalized. However, in attempting to distinguish broad groups of stakeholders rather than stakeholders in general, our aim has been for a range of voices and interests among the universities' publics to be represented and to try to avoid the dominance of the views of any one group. Arguably, the framing of public understanding of teaching excellence has been ideologically driven through the influence of government policy rhetoric constructed around market competition as a tool to drive quality. This ideological location and continuing policy trajectory move the sector in a particular direction, 'away from a civic to a market-driven agenda' (O'Leary and Wood, 2019: 125). How well suited is this agenda to the purposes of improving teaching quality? O'Leary and Wood (2019: 135–6) take the view that 'In the case of teaching, the TEF [in the UK] is the latest example of a sector-wide policy that is purportedly aimed at improving the quality of teaching and increasing student choice in HE, yet in reality is ill equipped to do either.'

The belief in competition and a market-driven approach as the means to improve quality and the 'increasing measurement paradigm of excellence' (Wood, 2017: 49) are contested and worthy of critical debate by stakeholders. The challenges for universities and the higher education curriculum in responding to government policies and the expectations and wants of different stakeholder groups are not to be underestimated, as made apparent by Barkas et al. (2019). There are 'students who want the knowledge to compete in the job markets, academic staff who have certain professional and personal/career requirements, employers who want to choose the best graduates for their own purposes and the government which endeavours to improve the country's prosperity and economic competitiveness by instigating drivers through its employability agendas' (Barkas et al., 2019: 804). It is timely and apposite to open up public debate about the wider purposes of higher education and teaching excellence, the environment and conditions necessary to engage higher education stakeholder constituencies in this, and thereby to consider other ways of seeing things and the possibility of change: 'And when it comes to change, what moves people is often not an argument from a principle, not a long discussion about values, but just a gradually acquired new way of seeing things' (Appiah, 2007: 73).

Higher Education as a Public Good and Civic Engagement

The idea of the civic university has taken many forms, as explored in this section, which are included to illustrate aspects of this heterogeneity and so that we can learn about the civic university from these contexts. The examples do not permit like-with-like comparisons to be drawn, but each is intrinsically interesting in its own right. The first, from the UK, provides some interesting historical context to the framing of the civic university. The second is from the Philippines, and its attempts to draw together academic excellence and social relevance suggest to us an alternative vision of 'academic excellence'.

Understandings of the role and wider purposes of higher education as a public good have been eroded in a market-led policy environment. Competition has impacted on higher education in the UK by creating division within the sector, leading to 'institutional stratification and the self-protective groupings of institutions which lobby intensively for their market niche' (Nixon, 2012: 12). What we have in the UK, Nixon argues, is a stratified higher education sector operating in an environment in which it makes sense for each institution or grouping of institutions to safeguard its own interests. Division and self-interest work against coordinated response across the sector to issues that cut across it (Nixon, 2012: 126). Similarly, different stakeholder groups may be divided by their different expectations and particular demands. We argue for more focus on commonality, and one way of working towards this is through reinstating the idea of higher education and the public good, which is greater than individual self-interest. There is a connectedness between quality and how we think about higher education's role in society (Brink, 2018), and in terms of developing inclusive critical understandings of teaching excellence in higher education, we argue that there is an important connection to the idea of the contemporary civic university. The difficulty in agreeing exactly what the civic university is refocuses attention not only on 'the deeply fundamental but complex question of "What are universities for?" but also suggests that leaders and managers need to ask themselves "What kind of a university do we want to be?" and need to understand the consequences for their institution in answering this question' (Kempton, 2016: 282).

Competition, market-led measures and changes in the funding regime have been among the key features of the policy reform agenda for higher education in England. Changes to the funding regime through the introduction of tuition fees and the student as consumer can be related to the 'general idea of consumer sovereignty' whereby, as Whitty explains, 'each individual is the best judge of his or her needs and wants, and of what is in their best interests'

(Whitty, 2002: 79–80). Today when 'increasingly, education is being treated as a private good rather than a public responsibility' (Whitty, 2002: 79), it can be useful to reflect on examples from other times and contexts.

There is 'an interesting history in the UK of linking civic engagement and higher education, which has been largely ignored in the present discussions of the purpose and future of higher education' (Annette, 2010: 454). While the idea of the 'civic university' may be more usually thought of as a reference to 'a small number of institutions in large English cities that have grown from nineteenth-century local university colleges with strong links to industry into current research-intensive universities' (Vallance, 2016: 16), the idea of the civic university can be applied more widely to many European universities having similar municipal roots and local ties, as Vallance argues, and, indeed, beyond Europe 'a rich civic tradition has marked higher education in the United States (US) from the nineteenth century' (Vallance, 2016: 16).

The civic university has its roots in history 'dating back to the nineteenth century in England and the United States of America (USA) particularly' (Goddard et al., 2016: 5). In the UK context, with reference to England, our discussion of the civic role of the university draws on the history of what are called the 'Redbrick' universities with their 'specific history pertaining to the civic university movement developed out of the modernist focus on industry and private funding' (Richardson, 2011: 119). 'Redbrick University' was a term coined by E. Allison Peers, writing under the pseudonym of 'Bruce Truscot', in his 1943 book. Silver (1999: 179) explains that 'At the time Peers was writing, in addition to Oxford, Cambridge, London and Durham, there were seven universities: Birmingham, Bristol, Leeds, Liverpool, Manchester, Reading and Sheffield.' Furthermore, Silver (1999: 179) continues: 'Truscot's redbrick universities had been created to provide opportunities in their cities for middle- and upper working-class families, and to further the industrial and commercial interests of their communities.' The University of Sheffield, for example, one of these seven universities, like others at the time had roots as civic colleges: 'Sheffield was one of a group of five, created from civic colleges, which received their charters in the first years of the twentieth century. They set out to educate the local workforce and were nurtured by the municipal pride of their city councils and by the ambitions of local manufacturers' (Mathers, 2005: 1). A strong public appeal among workers and residents in Sheffield helped to establish the University. An interesting question is the extent to which universities today may be defined by their origins. The 'redbrick' or 'civic' universities had a 'symbiotic relationship with the urban area which created them' (Mathers, 2005: 1), evident, for example, in the ties between the university, local people and industry. It also serves to illustrate the idea of connection to place (see Goddard et al., 2016).

The interrelationship of the idea of the civic university, the role of stakeholders and globalization is interesting to consider. Held (2010: 28) suggests that 'Globalization has become the "big idea" of our times', best understood as 'the widening, intensifying, speeding up and growing impact of worldwide interconnectedness' (Held, 2010: 29). It can be considered to embrace distinct types of change (Held, 2010: 29) and in relation to economic, cultural and political aspects, all being interrelated (Olssen, Codd and O'Neill, 2004: 4). The growing emphasis placed on world rankings of universities can be seen as a form of globalization (Vallance, 2016: 28), and this can be related to increased competition in higher education as part of the architecture of neoliberalism, as 'increased competition represents improved quality within neoliberalism' (Olssen, Codd and O'Neill, 2004: 187). In the origins of civic universities, there is often a connection to locality: local people and local industry. The connections of universities today are global and national as well as local: for example, universities may 'talent spot' and recruit international academic talent to their staff; they may have overseas campuses; and the constituency of the student body is drawn more widely now too, nationally and internationally. Furthermore, rankings have been a 'game changer' for the world of higher education, creating 'a storm which has blown around the world' Hazelkorn (2015: 222) and have 'changed the way we think about higher education, and the many characteristics of excellence' (pp. 222-3). Universities must attract students to secure funding, and their relationships with stakeholders today exist within a very different operating climate in which the idea of education as a public good has been displaced by a conception of education as serving self-interested consumers. The public good traditionally has been seen as that which was good for the locality and the nation (Nixon, 2012: 64) and some universities do recruit a significant proportion of their undergraduate students from within the broad region (Nixon, 2012: 64).

Changes to the ways universities are funded and a competitive market environment mean that universities embrace a business model. One thing successful businesses would argue is that an important component of their success is knowing, understanding, communicating and engaging well with their customers and stakeholders. Arguably, therefore, if universities are following the logic of being successful businesses and embracing the business model, they will engage well with their stakeholders. It can be argued that organizations and institutions engage with their stakeholders primarily to identify and establish what needs and desires they have and how these might then be matched with the services and functions provided. The kind of stakeholder analyses commonly employed by organizations in their planning seek to clarify what the organization offers, who comprises its market and what the needs of that market might be. In a market environment, engagement is about both understanding what customers want and developing demand for products and services. These approaches are rooted in a deficit and needs-based model. In other contexts, such as community development and health improvement, in both the public and third sectors, an asset-based, appreciative approach rooted in strengths and capabilities and the intrinsic worth of people and place is in evidence (Garven, McLean and Pattoni, 2016: 25). In relating this approach to both organizational practice and wider questions of democratic renewal and citizen participation, they argue that such an asset-based, appreciative approach has commonality with participatory democracy, in that both recognize inherent strengths in people and communities and seek to engage stakeholders as active citizens who shape and control communities and the services that affect and improve lives. The values and principles that underpin this approach to community and stakeholder engagement views people as co-producers rather than recipients of services and seeks to empower communities to create resources and develop and control provision of services. According to Garven, McLean and Pattoni (2016: 35), this approach to engagement is advocated by the World Health Organization and informs a range of community health and health improvement initiatives in the UK.

Going beyond location, the redbrick relationship to place speaks of a tradition of civic and public involvement. The present time may be an opportunity for universities to re-engage with the local, as part of 'building back better' in a post-pandemic world. For Carr and Hartnett (1996: 191), 'any democratic vision of education will be committed to fostering a wide public debate in which educational policies and proposals can be tested through critical dialogue and in which all can participate irrespective of occupational status or technical expertise'. The perspectives set out in the previous chapters have important contributions to make to critical dialogue and public debate about teaching excellence, and this might be enacted in a variety of ways. For example, stakeholder engagement and public debate might interact with the governance of universities, making them more democratic through increased openness to influences from a range of stakeholder voices and perspectives. Obviously, the examples of wider stakeholder engagement could be different for institutions in different contexts. The important point here is that institutions need to have a commitment to the wider stakeholder engagement on some of the key issues such as teaching quality and university civic missions.

Framing this discussion more widely in an international context, Nebres' account of his experiences of university leadership (2017) is drawn on. It provides interesting insights into how Ateneo de Manila University, a Catholic university in the Philippines, directly engages with and serves its local communities in an Asian context. Links between the university and local communities are apparent in many different ways in this context in relation to particular needs, such as from social, health and educational perspectives. Nebres' account provides examples of the university engaging with local government and communities to address issues of poverty and inequality. The practices and institutional responses described appear as a further illustration of the connection to place, local needs and the university's civic mission. It offers illustrations of university links between teaching, research, social engagement and civic purpose, and from examples of Ateneo de Manila University's direct engagement with the local community, the social relevance and importance of the university is apparent. For example, in the 1990s, Ateneo de Manila University attempted to bring academic excellence and social relevance together in its institutional structure and curriculum design. The University created the School of Medicine and Public Health in 1997. It addressed the national need because

> the major health problems of the Philippines were in the area of public health: tuberculosis, malaria, schistosomiasis, gastrointestinal diseases, bad sanitation and lack of clean drinking water. Having a School of Medicine and Public Health together would bridge the problematic divide in the

country between the culture of the medical profession and that of public health. (Nebres, 2017: 84)

In 1995, the University established the Ateneo Center for Educational Development (ACED). It aimed to improve educational achievement in public schools, where the majority of Filipino children study and where academic achievement was low and resources inadequate (p. 85). Guided by the findings of a study by Ateneo for the Philippine Department of Education in 1994, stakeholders (the principal, teachers, parents, pupils and community leaders) were brought together 'to work towards major academic improvement'. Working with teachers and partners the university engaged with initiatives to help address the effects of poverty on education and homelessness. For example, to address the issue of poverty in local communities, the university partnered with an organization which built homes and communities for 'the poorest of the poor' and over time built communities with about 800 families. Faculty members and students continue to work with these communities, particularly in helping the children and youth finish school (pp. 85–6).

This example from the Philippines illustrates how research, teaching and social engagement with stakeholders to help alleviate poverty and to meet the needs of communities are brought together through the university's civic purpose. The pursuit of teaching excellence from stakeholders' perspectives may be thought of in terms of curricula and teaching to promote socially engaged learning and 'employability' – the latter understood as concerned with 'learning that has benefits for citizenship, continued learning and life in general' (Knight and Yorke, 2004: 8), as discussed in Chapter 5. Reflecting on this example from a university in the Philippines offers some insights into how teaching excellence might be considered to include teaching that promotes civically and publicly involved learning.

Democratization of Teaching Excellence through Public Conversation

Appiah uses the word 'conversation' as a metaphor for the wider engagement with others (Appiah, 2007). The starting point for this book was a call for understandings about higher education, its purposes and the discourse of teaching excellence to be democratized and reshaped through civic debate with universities' stakeholder publics. This will require a genuine commitment to the challenges of different views, for 'Superficial consensus is relatively easy to achieve provided that differences are kept to a minimum and inconvenient disagreements are conveniently sidelined' (Nixon, 2012: 45), and to safeguard against what Bohm (2004: 10) referred to as *fragmentation* in thought, which he described as 'thought which divides everything up'. Such thought divides and separates things out, whereas through dialogue, Bohm explains, the aim is to 'suspend your opinions and to look at the opinions – to listen to everybody's opinions, to suspend them, and to see what all that means' (Bohm, 2004: 30). Through such a process, Bohm explains, a '*common content* is shared'. Understanding then moves beyond opinions and 'into something new and creative' (p. 32).

Writing with reference to American society, Putnam (2001) examined the weakening of community bonds and identified a need 'to create new structures and policies (public and private) to facilitate renewed civic engagement' (Putnam, 2001: 403). This book has argued for connections to be built between stakeholder perspectives and to work towards realization of the possibility of reconnecting higher education with the public (see Nixon, 2012: 118). Some issues raised by stakeholders in Chapters 2, 3, 4, 5 and 6 may offer possible starting points for conversations: for example, the wider benefits and intrinsic value of degree study, in addition to anticipated graduate career advantage; how the language works to shape understandings of roles in and responsibilities for teaching excellence; how non-numerical, qualitative, impalpable aspects of teaching excellence might be recognized; and the connection of teaching excellence with student learning. In arguing for possibilities and opportunities for stakeholders, as the universities' 'publics', to shape and reform the dominant discourse of teaching excellence, we have recognized some of the barriers and challenges. The language of teaching excellence, conjoined with that of market transactions between the higher education 'provider' and the 'consumer', is an example of an impediment to the construction of alternative understandings of the purposes of higher education and the discourse of teaching excellence: 'The language of higher education – the language used, that is, to explain and communicate the educational processes associated with higher education – has become increasingly bureaucratic, managerial and exclusive. It collapses all human reasoning into the kind of reasoning whose "outcomes" can be "pre-specified" with reference to specific "targets" (Nixon, 2012: 128). Higher education policy discourse employs terminology which, as we have examined with reference to Collini's (2012: 95) work, can 'colonize our minds'. As such, it can become internalized and accepted unquestioningly, and academics 'feel obliged to speak an alien language' (2012: 94).

As 'the dominance of certain discourses affects how an issue is understood and also helps to establish certain boundaries on the possibilities and limits of debate' (Forrester and Garratt, 2016: 11), so we suggest that how the dominant discourse of teaching excellence operates influences how the idea is understood, the language with which it is spoken about and how it is enacted. Finding a language to capture 'activities whose justification goes beyond instrumental purposes', as Collini explains (2012: 94), is an important and challenging task. The Teaching Excellence Framework (TEF) for example, as Brink (2018: 138) notes, is about 'the teaching provided to students, not about any growth in their learning'. Furthermore, TEF is concerned with proxies: 'teaching as proxy for learning, student satisfaction as proxy for quality of education, employment destination as proxy for learning gain' (Brink, 2018: 138). Attempting to make teaching excellence meaningful to public scrutiny through proxies and rankings is problematic. Our point is that public debate needs to reach beyond the proxies and rankings to the 'underlying conditions'. Reducing and limiting teaching excellence to specific metrics omits immeasurable, intangible aspects including, for example, relational aspects of the learning process.

Arguably, engaging stakeholders in debates about teaching excellence and the wider purposes of higher education may help to forge stronger links between universities, their communities and wider society, while being mindful of the risks of simplistic assumptions and the need for clarity when referring to the civic university and 'serving its community' (see Brink, 2018: 316). Furthermore, it can be argued that 'positioning yourself as a civic university will bring you no benefit whatsoever in terms of rankings and league tables' (Brink, 2018: 314). There is a 'growing obsession' worldwide with university rankings, which represent 'a manifestation of what has become known as the worldwide "battle for excellence". Rankings are 'perceived and used to determine the status of individual institutions, assess the quality and performance of the higher education system and gauge global competitiveness' (Hazelkorn, 2015: 1). This appears to dominate public debate. Arguably, in this climate there is a need for 'open and honest debate as to how best to democratise excellence for the good of the university sector as a whole' (Nixon, 2007: 30) and for this debate to engage minority and under-represented perspectives. 'Inclusive teaching excellence' has been referred to, denoting an idea of teaching excellence that is not imbued with Westernized assumptions and avoids totalizing notions; that recognizes diversity and the plurality of the public domain; holds fast to the principles of equity, fairness and collegiality; and affords primacy to the importance of learning relationships within pedagogic practice. Reference to 'an inclusive perspective' affirms a commitment to engaging with understandings situated in the diverse experiences and contexts of the plurality of stakeholder publics. Teaching excellence may look and feel quite different depending, for example, on positioning, experiences of higher education and social and cultural contexts.

Conclusion

Nixon (2012: 134) has argued that 'the great challenge facing higher education is to re-locate itself at the centre of civic society', and likewise this chapter has conceptualized engagement of universities with their stakeholders in public debate about teaching excellence as part of this role. This is a different kind of debate from what Carr and Harnett (1996: 191) refer to as 'the ideologically driven debate that has accompanied recent educational reforms', and it is the kind of debate advocated in this chapter to democratize understandings of teaching excellence and support new understandings. Opportunities to contribute to debate may need to be found, or they may already exist, and could include increased stakeholder participation in governance; in discussion and consultative groups; in employers' forums; and in other public engagement activities. The stakeholder perspectives included in the central chapters of the book offer ideas for approaches to developing inclusive debate about teaching excellence. For example, the pedagogical partnership approach, Students as Learners and Teachers (SaLT), in which Cook-Sather and Des-Ogugua (2019) drew on conversations which included students from under-represented groups. This illustrated an approach to engaging students' understandings of their lived experiences which informed recommendations to develop inclusive and responsive classrooms. The 'student as consumer' narrative is counteracted in examples of students conceptualized as 'partners', positioning them in a more active and engaged role. Cook-Sather and Des-Ogugua (2019) showed how inclusive and responsive classrooms can be created through engaging in 'ongoing processes of reflection and revision, ideally in collaboration with other faculty members and with students' (p. 605). This book has argued for inclusive civic debate with stakeholder publics, so that their voices may inform and reshape the dominant discourse on teaching excellence. Creating the conditions to draw stakeholder voices into this public debate presents challenges, yet is vital for the development of inclusive, democratic understandings of the purposes of higher education, to which issues of teaching excellence are integral.

The following discussion points captured in the box below arise from the examination of stakeholders' perspectives in this book.

Points for Discussion

- How might stakeholder perspectives be represented in the governance of higher education institutions?
- How might we learn from different contexts and times to think about teaching excellence?
- What might inclusive perspectives on teaching excellence look like in practice in a particular context?
- How might the conditions to engage critical public debate about teaching excellence which reaches beyond the proxies and rankings be created?

Coda

Teaching Excellence in Challenging Times

The last part of this book was written during the global Covid-19 pandemic in 2020 and 2021. The crisis of the pandemic has provided us with an opportunity to review and renew our understandings of teaching excellence. The pandemic seems unlikely to end soon and even when things return to a situation that we might recognize as more 'normal', some of the changes made during the pandemic may become embedded as part of the 'new normal'. This Coda draws together some reflections about teaching excellence in challenging times.

The repercussions of the Covid-19 pandemic have been felt across all areas of our lives, including higher education. One strand of our thinking in this book has been the influence of marketization on the higher education sector and universities operating as businesses. Arguably the pandemic has brought some of the weaknesses of this into full view: 'the pandemic has exposed the impact of 20 years of turning higher education into a marketplace and students into increasingly dissatisfied customers,' suggested Moore (2021) in an article discussing the impact of the pandemic on universities now operating in a marketized environment, and on students' experiences of university. How this manifests itself in the UK context – for example, students seeking rent refunds and fee reductions – and universities' responses to these demands has become apparent.

In 2020, the rapid move to online learning and teaching as the norm has presented challenges for staff and students and has required academics to become far more conversant and able as e-pedagogues:

> Education, across the board, has experienced drastic changes to teaching delivery. Transition into online learning has occurred rapidly and has presented a range of novel challenges both to staff and students. As noted by Burki (2020), the utilization of virtual learning may well persist until a

suitable vaccine for Covid-19 has been developed. (Burns, Dagnall and Holt, 2020: 6)

The implications of this rapid transition to online learning were huge for academics and students and the experience for individuals was varied, depending, for example, on factors such as, but not limited to, access to the requisite technology, bandwidth, available study space, childcare and homeschooling responsibilities and, as Burns, Dagnall and Holt (2020) note, the vast array of technological platforms to be navigated. Not only that, the isolation and lack of social contact have taken a toll. For staff, for example, while the 'virtual coffee morning' and other online socializing events have created opportunities for virtual 'meet ups' for social interactions, 'it is not the same as the coffee machine or coffee shop discussion with colleagues, let alone the Friday afternoon social get togethers. It clearly impacts on productivity, creativity and mental wellbeing' (Goedegebuure and Meek, 2021: 3). For many students, physical isolation has been keenly felt during 'lockdown' and while opportunities for face-to-face socialization in a physical classroom or lecture hall with peers have been severely curtailed, academics have made use of 'breakout groups', the 'chat' function and the many online tools for students to work collaboratively, often deploying these in the online learning environment to stimulate interactivity and shared learning with peers.

In this book we have argued for the development of inclusive understandings of teaching excellence and an added dimension to this is what inclusive teaching excellence may mean in 'the post-coronial university', a term used by Eringfled (2021) 'to signify the re-imagined university both during and after the pandemic' (p. 148). The pandemic has thrown health and wealth inequalities into sharper relief; for example, a review by Public Health England (2020) of disparities in the risk and outcomes of Covid-19 showed 'an association between belonging to some ethnic groups and the likelihood of testing positive and dying with Covid-19', as not all population groups are affected equally by Covid-19 (p. 4). Some of the ways in which the pandemic has laid bare inequalities and the unequal impact of the Covid-19 virus were evident in the report which noted that 'Ethnic inequalities in health and wellbeing in the UK existed before Covid-19 and the pandemic has made these disparities more apparent and undoubtedly exacerbated them' (p. 8).

The Covid-19 pandemic and its effects on employment prospects for so many people, including graduates, in the post-industrial, post-Covid graduate labour market adds another dimension to debates about graduate employability, which were explored in Chapter 5. In the UK context, the Office for Students (OfS) annual review (2020) reported that 'current graduate employment prospects are extremely uncertain. The coronavirus pandemic and lockdowns have resulted in a severe economic contraction. Many businesses have gone into administration and many more have instigated a hiring freeze. The impact is likely to be geographically uneven and long-lasting' (p. 53). Also, the effects of the UK exit from the European Union (Brexit) on the economy, the labour market and availability of graduate job opportunities in the immediate and the longer term seem uncertain.

Inclusive Curricula and Teaching Excellence

Shocking and tragic media reports of the appalling legacy and continued impact on people and communities of historic and structural racism and inequalities entrenched in societies have gained media prominence during 2020. Entrenched and continuing issues of social justice, fairness, the operation of power and whose voices have been marginalized and overlooked, surfaced and gained expression through activism and protest. This has provoked debate and has challenged assumptions and attitudes. Elias et al. (2021) refer to emerging research indicating an increase in racism and xenophobia in the coronavirus pandemic which, as they note, is set against 'a backdrop of rising nationalism and populism spreading worldwide over the last two decades' (p. 1). The challenges of nationalism, populism and xenophobia reinforce the crucial point that teaching excellence must guard against Eurocentricism. A commitment to inclusion of minority voices and perspectives, for example, motivates efforts to decolonize the curriculum, examining the scholarship underpinning it, the cultural assumptions on which this is based and whose perspectives are represented. Inclusive approaches to teaching excellence also embody a commitment to listening to students in order to understand how to enhance their educational experiences (Harper and Quaye, 2009) and classroom approaches such as pedagogical partnership work. This can be challenging but may support inclusive teaching excellence with potential for such work to contribute to inclusive practice which is 'responsive to the multiple and diverse voices and experiences of staff and students' (Cook-Sather, 2020: 898). Mercer-Mapstone et al. (2021: 227) note that 'Teaching and learning in higher education (HE) must evolve to be able to meet the needs of increasingly diverse student cohorts in equitable ways.' Inclusive teaching excellence recognizes diversity and the importance of decolonizing the higher education curriculum, divesting it of Eurocentricism and 'the centrality of Whiteness as an instrument of power and privilege' such that particular types of knowledge are not privileged while others are absent (Arday, Belluigi and Thomas, 2021: 298).

In an era of 'fake news' and 'alternative facts', we are reminded that the development of critical faculties and intellectual challenge have great importance for excellent teaching and learning in higher education. The importance of opportunities to engage in debate is part of the ethos of higher education. The events surrounding the transition of power in the US presidential election in 2021 highlight the very real way in which fake news and mendacity as accepted public discourse are a threat to democracy. The development of critical thinking and critical literacy, integral to higher learning, supports students to become critically discerning, able to judge the credibility of source material and the veracity of claims. The role of critical information literacy is important as it 'challenges the traditional conceptions of good and bad information, and compels students to ask not only if information is reliable, truthful and trustworthy, but also what or whose cause it serves, the context in which it arose, and who may be disadvantaged by it' (Georgiadou et al., 2018: section 2.2). Support for this could be advanced through collaboration between academic staff and librarians (Georgiadou et al., 2018: section 2.2).

This book has argued that for the development of inclusive understandings of teaching excellence, it requires each stakeholder group to be invited to the table and for the diverse publics within each group to be given a voice. For Arendt (1958) the significance of the public realm is that it is common to all of us and therefore all should have the opportunity of being seen and heard by others. It is the reality of the public realm that it 'relies on the simultaneous presence of innumerable perspectives and aspects in which the common world presents itself and for which no common measurement or denominator can ever be devised' (p. 57). In such a state of plurality Arendt suggests that the idea of the table to which all are invited is a world of things in common which 'relates and separates men (*sic*) at the same time' (p. 52) and this allows plurality to function and all to be seen and heard, or as Arendt puts it, 'prevents our falling over each other'.

Making this plurality function requires inclusive conceptions of teaching excellence that must engage the perspectives of Black, Asian and Minority Ethnic (BAME) students and other under-represented groups. Bringing these and other marginalized voices to the Arendtian table to enter into dialogue about teaching excellence in higher education is central to the development of an inclusive view. This also brings to the fore the importance of widening participation to engage students from under-represented groups and of ensuring that approaches 'move beyond sameness to customize educational practices and maximize engagement and outcomes for all' (Harper and Quaye, 2009: 12). The extent and impact of inequality highlighted by the pandemic and the damage to young people's life chances suggest that a renewed focus on widening participation in this way is an important component of 'building back better' post-pandemic. Inclusive teaching excellence is coexistent with curricula that are not dominated by Eurocentric assumptions that privilege certain types of knowledge and fail to represent and validate others: 'The monopoly and proliferation of dominant White European canons comprises much of our existing curriculum and consequently impacts adversely on Black, Asian and Minority Ethnic (BAME) learners' engagement and sense of belonging' (Arday, Belluigi and Thomas, 2021: 298). The recent campaigns and movements (both on and off campus) such as Rhodes Must Fall and Black Lives Matter have provided a powerful reminder of the rich history, activity, scholarship and context of de-colonization of the curriculum, what Said (1994: 36) calls the 'whole movement, literature, and theory of resistance and response to empire'. This movement to decolonize both the curriculum and the mind has a long pedigree and provides substantial foundations for rebuilding both the curriculum and institutions of higher education in ways that expose and confront the worldwide pattern and impact of imperialism and illuminate the historical and contemporary resistance against empire and colonialism. Such a shift in thinking and organization is necessary to demonstrate that institutions and individuals in the sector are serious about dialogue and listening to and hearing a plurality of voices. The importance of listening to stakeholder understandings in constructions of teaching excellence has been emphasized in this book.

The term 'inclusive' is understood in different ways as recognized by Lawrie et. al (2017), who find the following definition of inclusive to provide an apt framing for their discussion: 'inclusive learning and teaching in higher education refers to the ways in which pedagogy, curricula and assessment are designed to engage students in learning that is meaningful, relevant, and accessible to all' (Hockings, 2010: 1 cited in Lawrie et al., 2017: 2). Student voice and partnership are often referred to by institutions in terms of strategies for student engagement, as noted in Chapter 2 and this book has called for the development of inclusive understandings that engage students and other stakeholder groups. The integrity of this project relates fundamentally to the genuineness of this inclusivity, and the words of Lygo-Baker et al. (2019) in their discussion of what they refer to as 'the single voice fallacy' seem to resonate with the importance and the challenges this brings:

> In a hierarchical system that is not used to engaging with a diversity of proactive voices, there is likely to be competition to be heard. As a consequence, there might be a number of 'lost voices', where the loss may be felt by individuals who feel marginalized, but also where loss represents missed opportunities for organisational learning. To avoid drowning in a sea of voices, universities may have developed selective hearing – where certain voices are allowed to become dominant over others, and the voice of the 'ruling stratum' becomes the accepted voice (Hobden & Wyn Jones, 2017, p. 138). This seems to run contrary to the widely espoused goals of diversity and inclusion. (Lygo-Baker, Kinchin and Winstone, 2019: 2)

In this volume the call for public debate has emphasized the need to avoid totalizing notions of the public. To be democratic, public debate must engage with the diverse nature of stakeholder groups and the points raised by Lygo-Baker, Kinchin and Winstone (2019) in the previous quote seem particularly apt. We have argued elsewhere (Wood and Su, 2017) for the importance of relational aspects within conceptualizations of teaching excellence and are aware of the need to consider how this translates into the 'post-coronial university' setting. Here models and practice of teaching and learning may look different, and relationships and learning encounters during the pandemic are often experienced as much in the virtual environment as in the physical world. The benefits for teaching and learning of positive relationships between students and their peers, and between students and academic staff, are examined by Bovill (2020). Listening to students is important in order to understand how to enhance their educational experiences (Harper and Quaye, 2009: 8) and student insights into teaching and learning may feed into co-design and co-creation of curricula with wider benefits, too, for students and academics (Cook-Sather et al., 2014 cited in Bovill, 2020: 35). Staff–student partnership can be understood as 'a collaborative, reciprocal process through which all participants have the opportunity to contribute equally, although not necessarily in the same ways, to curricular or pedagogical conceptualization, decision-making, implementation, investigation, or analysis' (Cook-Sather et al, 2014: 6–7, cited in Bovill, 2020: 28). Partnership approaches that do not just engage already engaged students (Bovill, 2020: 39) are important for inclusive understandings to emerge and teaching excellence to develop. Staff–student partnership approaches can bring a number of benefits and can contribute to the creation of spaces for exclusionary practices to be countered (Mercer-Mapstone, Islam and Reid, 2021). However, there are challenges, for example, when it is engagement only with the students who are already engaged, for as Mercer-Mapstone et al. note, students most likely to participate in partnership work are the elite (p. 220).

The benefits of working in partnership with a student consultant are evident in an account by Perez (2016) of her practice as a recently appointed physics professor. Perez explains her own positioning as 'a mixed-race White and Hispanic woman from a low-income urban area'. She explains that as a student herself in similar classrooms, she

> had a nagging knowledge that silent factors were keeping others like me away from physics and that any level of success I achieved would be an exception to the norm. I wanted to openly address similar concerns among these students, not only to relieve the anxiety of those who felt they did not belong, but also to encourage everyone to consider how their actions shape the academic community they are joining. (p. 1)

Perez worked with a student consultant, 'herself an underrepresented student who had been dissuaded from a STEM field by her experience in undergraduate classes' (p. 2). Weekly meetings between the two provided space for reflective dialogue, and working in partnership, strategies were identified to develop classroom practice. For example, Perez refers to the creation of a 'brave space', understood in two senses. First, in the sense of making time to reflect on values and the development of teaching practices. Second, the 'brave space' is understood in the sense that

> the relationship supported the 'bravery' needed to question the traditional boundaries of what is discussed in an undergraduate physic class. Whereas many humanities classes can encourage critique of which authors are included or excluded from a syllabus and why, or how societal factors influence the construction of a canon, the self-view of physics as a linear accumulation of objectively-necessary skills, and of success in physics as based solely on aptitude in these skills, can restrict discussion of social issues in the classroom. (p. 2)

Another example was a 'first-day feedback form for all new classes, where students are asked their preferred name and pronouns and given space to tell me about their values and goals for the course'. Although small, these changes can convey powerful messages and influence the relational climate and learning environment of the classroom: 'These are minor changes, but by going over these documents during the first day of class, I hope to communicate to vulnerable students that I strive to be an ally whom they can turn to for support and to all students that they are accountable for the classroom environment that we create' (p. 4). Working with a student consultant in partnership 'was essential for developing the brave space necessary to have these conversations, validating how my personal experiences influence my teaching, and supporting the changes I attempt to make' (p. 5).

Inclusive curricula for teaching excellence are grounded in practices that respond to and validate diverse perspectives and needs, as demonstrated through Perez' account and in the following example from a university in the United States. This also recognizes the need to include a diversity of perspectives which go beyond the dominance of a canon of White male authors, and the creation of an inclusive learning environment in the classroom.

What Might Inclusive Curricula Look Like in Practice?

Many universities pay attention to the issue of inclusive curricula, including some of the elite universities. At Yale University in the United States, inclusive teaching is seen as a pedagogy that strives to serve the needs of all students, regardless of background or identity, and supports their engagement with their learning.

> Its inclusive teaching strategies are separated into the following two categories: (1) incorporating diverse perspectives into course content by expanding reading lists beyond White male authors, offering various ethnic and racial perspectives in case studies, ensuring teaching materials offer a variety of human examples and avoiding tokenizing particular individuals, students or representations; and (2) creating an inclusive classroom climate where all students are encouraged to participate, by learning about students' backgrounds and tailoring approaches accordingly, establishing ground rules for discussing controversial issues, and developing deeper racial and socio-economic awareness.
>
> To implement these strategies, the university recommends that academics consider various approaches in the learning and teaching process, for example, providing student support in and out of the classroom; considering a teaching and learning framework to enhance accessibility for diverse student bodies; examining implicit biases in the learning and teaching process; maintaining awareness of classroom diversity and understanding of various racial and socio-economic factors in their classes; incorporating diversity into the curriculum in order to represent diverse types of perspectives through course content and materials; adding a diversity statement to the syllabus that outlines the teaching philosophy and classroom ground rules for respectful classroom discussions and an inclusive learning community; considering universal design for learning (UDL) principles to enable varied and comprehensive access of course content to all students; soliciting student feedback and addressing any inclusivity concerns in a timely manner; reviewing the literature to learn more about critical pedagogies and texts on diversity in education in their subject area (Yale University Poorvu Center for Teaching and Learning, 2020).

Care and Relation-based Pedagogy

Research shows that relationships impact considerably upon students' experiences of higher education – meaningful connections with tutors are crucial (Felten and Lambert, 2020). Palmer (1983: xvi, cited in Bovill, 2020: 1) reminds us that 'real learning does not happen until students are brought into relationship with the teacher; with each other; and with the subject. We cannot learn deeply and well until a community of learning is created in the classroom'. Bovill (2020) suggests that relational pedagogy puts relationships at the heart of teaching and emphasizes that a meaningful connection needs to be established between teacher and students as well as between students and their peers, if effective learning is to take place.

Relationships matter especially for those who are traditionally marginalized in higher education. In their study in America, Felten and Lambert (2020: 17) uncovered four interlocking relationship-rich principles that guide both effective programmes and generative cultures at colleges and universities: (1) every student must experience genuine welcome and deep care; (2) every student must be inspired to learn; (3) every student must develop a web of significant relationships; and (4) every student must explore questions of meaning and purpose. Students are primary actors in all four of these principles but higher education institutions need to provide the conditions in which they can develop relationships, ask questions and advance their learning. The authors have also highlighted some of the challenges in creating institutional conditions to foster a culture of relationship-driven pedagogy. For example, the research mission dominates everything else. In addition, heavy teaching loads and a largely adjunct workforce make it difficult for academics to connect meaningfully with their students.

There are practical ways to foster relationships between academics and students for the purposes of learning – for example, learning a student's name. It is simple but impactful; prioritizes time for student conversations in one-to-one meetings; and deepens relationships through tutor or peer mentoring.

A form of mentoring in higher education is mentoring of students by their personal tutor (Yale, 2020). Mentoring can be defined as 'a relationship between two people with learning and development as its purpose' (Megginson and Garvey, 2004: 2 cited in Brockbank and McGill, 2007: 318). A common understanding of mentoring in higher education is a sustained relationship between a scholar and a protégé (Felten and Lambert, 2020). Both definitions centre on a relationship, and building a positive student–personal tutor relationship, as Yale (2020) suggests, brings benefits and positive outcomes for students, personal tutors and the institution. In many higher education institutions in the UK there are systems of personal tutoring and academic advising in place where the personal tutor/academic advisers practice this care-based relational approach. A wide range of personal tutoring systems exist in higher education institutions in the UK (Thomas, 2006: 25 drawing on the work of Owen, 2002) and practice in personal tutoring may differ across and within institutions (Yale, 2020). Drawing on the three broad models of personal tutoring outlined by Earwaker, of pastoral, professional and curricular approaches (Earwaker, 1992, cited in Yale, 2020), Yale suggests that the pastoral approach is most prevalent across institutions and that it is the more personal and pastoral approaches to personal tutoring that incorporate the skills of the mentor (pp. 77–8). Personal tutoring systems are often the personal face of the university for students, providing them with a one-to-one relationship with someone who is interested in them and who they feel confident will be a good source of support and guidance. There is a positive correlation between student satisfaction with the personal tutoring they receive and the learning outcomes and overall satisfaction with the educational experience (Grey and Osborne, 2020: 287). Personal tutoring works on the basis of a relationship with someone who takes an interest in the students and to whom they are known as individuals.

The Covid-19 pandemic has changed the landscape of higher education in profound ways. As Burns, Dagnall and Holt (2020) noted in their study of UK universities and the impact of the pandemic on student well-being: 'In the United Kingdom, universities have moved to close their campuses to both students and non-essential staff in an effort to protect them from contracting the virus. The repercussions of these decisions have been monumental for the delivery of teaching, relationships and, importantly, the provision of student services.' The pandemic has added another significant dimension to the wide range of potential stresses and difficulties students in higher education may encounter, such as the stresses of adolescence, and leaving home and family, as they transition to university and where 'some quickly adapt, make new friends and settle in, whereas others feel isolated and lonely without the ready support of family and friends' (Wheeler and Birtle, 1993: 3). Making friends and settling in has not been aided by the pandemic, with periods of 'lockdown' and loss of opportunities for social interaction. Relationships have been described as 'the beating heart of the undergraduate experience' (Felten and Lambert, 2021: 1) and developing a positive Personal Tutor (PT) relationship in the first year of university is linked to many positive student outcomes (Yale, 2019: 533). The PT role may combine responsibility for academic and pastoral support through the provision of guidance or referral to appropriate services (McFarlane, 2016: 78), and 'personal tutors' are defined by McFarlane as 'academic members of staff or faculty whose role is to provide this support to students, with a view to fostering their engagement in learning'(McFarlane, 2016: 78). The relationship at the heart of the academic and personal support provided by the personal tutor is an important one for, as Grey and Osborne (2020: 287) note:

> The evidence suggests that fostering belonging is critical to student engagement particularly in the first year of the university experience (McFarlane, 2016) and that developing a relationship with a member of academic staff in their discipline or programme of study enables students to feel more connected. (Thomas, 2012)

Dialogue about role expectations and responsibilities may help to build a more equal and positive student–personal tutor relationship, as Yale (2020) notes and suggests that personal tutors should be encouraged to engage in 'open, constructive communication and discussion with students, which would serve to provide a more equal relationship and rebalance the power in the relationship from the perceived authority of the personal tutor towards mutual collaboration between parties' (Yale, 2020: 88). Experiences of isolation and disconnection during the pandemic in particular may bring the importance and significance of the personal tutor–student relationship and the support and guidance of the personal tutor to the fore.

A care and relation-based pedagogy is also relevant to the practice of collegiality among academics, particularly during the pandemic. In a study conducted by the American Educational Research Association (AERA) and the Spencer Foundation on the impact of the Covid-19 pandemic on early career scholars and doctoral students in the US context, the authors (Levine et al., 2021) invited focus group participants to use two words that captured their feelings and experiences of working during the pandemic. Words such as 'anxious', 'worried', 'stressed', 'chaotic', 'unsettled', 'upheaval', 'exhausted', 'tired' and 'challenged' emerged. A participant working in a research-intensive university reflected (p. 7):

> And I guess my two words would be 'overwhelmed', because there is a lot happening, it seems, all at once, and my inbox is ridiculous every morning, even more so than it was before. It's usually very bittersweet for me when the semester ends and we have graduation, and this particular end of this semester, I'm just so happy it's over.

Care for others requires that academics also care for themselves and be mindful of the needs of colleagues. Jung (2015) argues that there is an inexorable and complementary quality to the relationship between self-care and care for others. 'It is inexorable in that they are not discrete; it is complementary in that each implies and requires the other' (p. 103). One of the critiques of the neoliberal university is that institutions need to show more care for their staff. For instance, precarious short-term contracts for academics in higher education often cause insecurity and uncertainty. This matters because staff on insecure contracts face a daily struggle to deliver a high level of professional service for students. Building relationships with students and others takes time. It is harder to achieve this while someone is on a precarious job contract.

The upheavals, uncertainties and anxieties experienced by many students during the time of the pandemic have raised awareness of the importance of feelings and emotions and of factoring these into thinking about teaching excellence. The influence of the learner's feelings on the learning process has implications for educators in creating learning environments. Schoper and Amelse (2020) refer to a 'new narrative' which recognizes the role of emotions in the learning process. They suggest that the 'old narrative' about emotions and learning dominant in Western culture 'is the belief that for learning to occur, emotions must be set aside' (p. 188). The new narrative, to which Schoper and Amelse (2020) refer, respects learners as co-creators of the learning process (p. 191). For example, they refer to designing learning experiences that start with what learners already know and build on the learner's existing neuronal networks: 'Neuronal networks are connected to the learners' lived experiences. Thus, the learner may share experiences the educator has not had or considered; being open to hearing such experiences and validating them is vital as doing so helps the educator to partner with the learner in their learning process' (p. 192). Factoring in the part played by emotions and relationships that validate the diverse experience of all learners, including marginalized students and those least well served and those under-represented in higher education, may represent a challenge to dominant outcomes-focused and metrics-driven conceptualizations of excellence in teaching and learning.

What Might a Care and Relation-based Pedagogy Look Like in Practice?

A relation-based pedagogy is often driven by genuine and deep care. One of the approaches to practising this is through tutor mentoring. Felten and Lambert (2020: 144) share a student's reflection on how two mentoring conversations led to her decision to pursue a career as a teacher in an American context. The student never imagined herself in education because she had struggled with ADHD throughout her years of schooling.

> First, Lisa Silverman, my psychology professor, said, 'Peta, your papers are terrific. Why don't you go into education?' I'm like, 'Me, teaching children? I can't teach anybody. I barely made it through school. I can't do that.' Professor Silverman replied, 'Think about it.' The next day I got a copy of an email from her to a professor in the education department. It said, 'I might have found you an excellent teacher candidate.' I decided to follow Professor Silverman's advice so I went to see Professor Cornelia in education, who told me she also had ADHD. She sat me down in her office and showed me all her credentials on her wall, and she said, 'I am you. And look where I am. You are going to be a great educator because you know what these kids are going through. You were that person in the back of the class that the teacher says can't do it.' And then she asked me to sit down in her chair behind her desk, and she said, 'You're in the professor's chair. That's your master's on the wall. That's your PhD. How are you going to tell me you can't do it? You're going to be a great teacher.'

The above scenario in which a student reflected on the influence of two mentoring conversations, demonstrates the power of dialogue to help dispel the negativity of the internal 'I can't' narrative – 'I can't teach anybody', 'I can't do that'. In this scenario, the demonstration of empathy and encouragement appeared pivotal in helping the student to overcome barriers such as an apparent lack of self-belief.

Mentoring conversations tend to have a profound impact on student's learning and development even long after the conversations took place. Sometimes it even transforms a student's way of being as illustrated in the following student's email to the second author of this book who taught the student as her personal tutor in an English university (Su and Wood, 2017: 30):

> I just wanted to let you know for the first time I really feel like I have made an informed decision when I voted this morning [the UK general election in 2015]

> and this is because of your education for all lectures. I took on board what you said and I contacted each of our local candidates, told them what was important to me and asked what their proposals were. I had replies and conversations with two of them and have read their local manifestos, I would never have done that both prior to your lectures and starting the course. I also stood as a parent governor for my son's school, again something I wouldn't have done, I didn't get elected but enjoyed having the opportunity.

The Pandemic and Blended Learning Pedagogy

The Covid-19 pandemic has fundamentally changed how universities approach learning and teaching. During the pandemic many universities shifted the majority of teaching online at short notice for both academics and students. Only a few face-to-face sessions were kept for workshops, laboratory practical work and studio work. As universities develop their exit strategies from the pandemic arrangements it may well be that this blend of online and face-to-face teaching remains in place in the foreseeable future. It is not an easy task because universities have traditionally privileged face-to-face teaching on campus. Blended learning pedagogy refers to teaching and learning conducted via a combination of face-to-face classroom learning and technology-based online learning approaches. While not diminishing the important demands and difficulties that online learning may present, in some ways it may be considered to be ideally placed to address many challenges caused by the Covid-19 pandemic, for a number of reasons. For example, these include the potential it offers to enhance and extend learning opportunities for students beyond the classroom setting, and the flexibility offered by asynchronous learning. However, beyond practical and pragmatic issues, it is important to think through the rationale and pedagogic justification for the blend of face-to-face and online learning.

Developing a blended learning model requires strong leadership and significant time commitment. Ultimately, whether universities fully explore the possibilities of blended learning depends on the adequacy of the resources committed to it. University leaders need to be mindful of not underestimating how much time and resources are needed to design and implement a successful blended learning programme. There is a need to dispel the myth that online learning is less resource-intensive in terms of demands on academics' time. For example, academics who are not familiar with the blended learning model may need to make time for professional development in this area.

On an operational level, a successful blended learning course requires detailed thinking on how the course is structured; the level of the 'blend' between face-to-face teaching and online learning; and course delivery strategies. Su and Beaumont (2010) found that the following strategies might contribute to the success of the blended learning course implementation. These strategies include integrating a variety of technologies; setting clear expectations at the beginning of the course, and later reminding students of these expectations; adopting a clear organizational system, organizing the course carefully and providing a syllabus and course outline; selecting active learning techniques; taking advantage of online resources and multimedia materials and integrating them into both the classroom and the e-learning lessons; offering collaborative learning options both in class and online; and using multiple assessment methods.

When designing assessment strategies for blended learning, academics need to consider incorporating digital technologies into the assessment process to enable timely feedback. For instance, tutors need to consider the use of the virtual learning environment (VLE) or other external online tools for assignment submission and provision of digital feedback such as rubrics, and audio/video feedback. For some blended learning courses aimed at professional learning, e-portfolios are often adopted as an assessment method.

In order to understand the response to Covid-19 and explore the future of digital learning and teaching, the Joint Information Systems Committee (JISC) conducted a sector-wide study with 439 students, 323 lecturers and 40 leaders in the UK in 2020. The study found that there were both challenges to, and benefits of, online learning experienced by students and academics.

On the students' experience, the authors of the JISC study (Maguire, Dale and M. Pauli, 2020: 11) found that

- Students like online learning mainly because it is more convenient, saves time, is more flexible and helps them to review content better.
- Enjoyment of online learning increases with experience of it – those for whom it has always been a large part of learning are much more likely to enjoy it than those with limited experience.

- Online learning can feel isolated and lonely when it lacks in-person social or human interactions.
- Students need access to the right kit – hardware, software, network connection and printer – and a conducive learning space.
- All students want to be more involved in how their course is delivered and the technology that is used for it.

Regarding the views of lecturers, the authors of the JISC study (Maguire, Dale and M. Pauli, 2020: 14) found that

- The level of online delivery is growing rapidly and blended learning is becoming the standard model for learning and teaching in UK higher education.
- Lecturers want and need to rethink learning and teaching practices to take advantage of advances in online learning approaches, especially as lecturers' confidence and awareness grow.
- Given the uncertainty created by Covid-19 and the speed of change, not surprisingly, lecturers would like increased clarity about their university's plans for delivering learning and teaching.
- Lecturers are under significant pressure to adapt and deliver online and blended learning and are often time-poor.
- But they are growing steadily more confident about delivering digitally.

There are a number of implications that we can draw from the above findings. One of them is that universities need to recognize and respond to the issues related to the digital divide and digital poverty. Some students from disadvantaged groups are more affected by digital poverty than others from more advantaged backgrounds. The Office of Students (OfS) suggests (2020) that digital poverty occurs when a student lacks access to one of the following: 'an appropriate device; good connectivity; reliable back-up when things go wrong; relevant software; a trained teacher; and space in which to work'. According to a September 2020 survey by OfS, during the lockdown 52 per cent of students said their learning was impacted by a slow or unreliable internet connection and 18 per cent were affected by lack of access to a computer, laptop or tablet device. For mature students and academics, family commitments such as homeschooling during the pandemic lockdowns have created additional pressure for working from home.

Another implication is students' and academics' skill sets required for online learning and teaching. Sometimes these skill sets are referred to as digital literacies. JISC (2014) defines digital literacies as 'those capabilities which fit someone for living, learning and working in a digital society'. In other words, digital literacy is the ability to locate, organize, understand, evaluate and analyse information using digital technology. It involves a working knowledge of current tools and an understanding of how they can be used. During the pandemic era, the development of students' and academics' digital literacies has become more urgent than ever as it underpins the success of online learning and teaching. Developing students' digital literacies is not just about learning the use of a particular device or software application, but it is also about developing the learners' confidence in their use of education technologies in general.

What Might Blended Learning Pedagogy Look Like in Practice?

During the Covid-19 pandemic, many universities in the UK adopted a blended learning pedagogy. A university situated in the north of England adopted a blended learning model for the majority of undergraduate and postgraduate provisions. It combined face-to-face synchronous online learning with asynchronous online learning. The traditional face-to-face teaching sessions were kept for a few degree subjects which have laboratory practical work and studio work. Lectures were pre-recorded with subtitles and made available in the university's virtual learning environment (VLE). Students were able to access and study the lecture materials in their own time. To consolidate students' learning, seminar and tutorial sessions were conducted online synchronously. The main tasks in the synchronous online sessions focused on the discussion of key concepts and reading associated with each week's lecture topics. This approach is often described as a 'flipped classroom'.

In the design of the blended learning model, the university paid close attention to the following considerations – developing a community of learning so that students have a sense of belonging to a community of learners; ensuring the tutor's presence in the virtual learning environment, such as engagement with students' contribution to online tasks and virtual office hours to provide students with additional support; structuring students' learning by communicating to students clearly about the learning tasks each week; and offering staff and students additional training on using educational technologies and providing additional computing equipment for those without ready access to a computer at home.

Lastly, the university also reviewed and revised the assessment strategies for the blended learning model. For instance, the traditional exams were replaced by timed online exams usually within a 24-hour window. In addition, e-portfolios as an assessment method was widely adopted to evidence students' learning with the potential for creativity and flexibility.

Conclusion

The Covid-19 pandemic has highlighted the importance of an inclusive perspective on teaching excellence, which requires greater attention to seeking out and having genuine dialogue with a diverse range of stakeholders in higher education. The pandemic has also highlighted certain aspects of teaching which are crucially important but not valued enough in current teaching excellence discourses. One theme threaded through the Coda has concerned the centrality of relationships. This theme of relationships has been brought to the fore during the pandemic when care and relationships with others have mattered so much. Another theme has been the importance of equity and inclusion within conceptions of teaching excellence. Some of the benefits and the importance of staff–student pedagogic partnerships that offer opportunities for all students to participate and which harness their insights to build inclusive understandings of teaching excellence in higher education have been illustrated. However, it is important that partnership approaches engage with diverse voices including those of students who feel marginalized. A further theme brought to the fore during the pandemic has been blended learning pedagogy which may also offer scope for more flexible and inclusive learning in a post-pandemic future, provided considerations such as equity and accessibility, for example, are addressed. An inclusive perspective on teaching excellence will help us to renew the promise of higher education as a public good.

Notes

Chapter 2

1 Nine of the institutions were considered to be research-intensive universities while the other nine were considered to be teaching-intensive universities. These research-intensive universities were all part of the Russell Group, which is a self-selected association of twenty-four public research universities in the UK. Most of the teaching-intensive universities were new universities, which gained their degree awarding powers after 1992. The university samples were randomly selected for the study. The sample was also purposive, with description rather than generalization being the aim (Dawson, 2007), and 'random purposeful' sampling (Creswell, 2007: 127) was used to make a random selection of a sample of eighteen from the list of seventy-six institutions awarded Gold. The narrative submissions are available on the Office for Students' website under the TEF section. For the purposes of anonymity, each of these institutions is given a code name. T1 to T9 represent teaching- intensive universities while R1 to R9 represent research-intensive universities. In this chapter, we report our findings from the analysis of how these institutions articulate teaching quality in relation to student engagement, valuing teaching, rigour and stretch, and feedback. We also explore if there are any differences in the articulation of teaching quality between research-intensive universities and teaching-intensive universities.

Chapter 3

1 The research participants were at different stages of their careers, ranging from postdoctoral teaching fellow to senior academics. In the interviews, participants were invited to share their understanding of the term 'teaching excellence' with suggested examples, and the measurability of it. Given the scale of the study, our sample of respondents ought not be considered representative. The findings

presented in the chapter should therefore be interpreted as being indicative of academics' perspectives on teaching excellence rather than definitive. To ensure anonymity of the respondents, they have been given a code name in this chapter.

Chapter 5

1   In order to explore understandings of employers' perspectives on teaching excellence in higher education to promote graduate employability, data was collected via email and telephone interview with seven careers advisors from four English universities. In addition, the views of a person with direct experience of the global world of business through a background as managing director of international consulting companies were included in our data set. Currently providing professional consultancy services to businesses and also as a professor at a UK Russell Group university, this respondent was well placed to offer a perspective from first-hand experience both of the business world and academia. Among the careers adviser respondents were those with specific roles in student placements and employer engagement. Email questions were sent to individual respondents and on receipt of their responses a supplementary question(s) was typically sent in order to probe particular ideas in more depth. We have therefore referred to this as an asynchronous email interview rather than a survey, as the follow-up questions included some interaction and engaged the participants to some extent in dialogic exchange. There may be benefits in terms of convenience as well as richness of the data when gathered asynchronously (Wood and Su, 2017; James and Busher, 2009) and through a text-based medium such as email. As James and Busher (2009: 28) suggest, 'email interviewing can at the very least generate more considered narratives and rich discourse that is reflective, analytical and creative, providing a depth that might be absent in uttered data'. The telephone interview by contrast is a synchronous method and one which it is suggested may yield 'detailed and considered replies of the kind typically sought by qualitative researchers' (Bryman, 2008: 458), and one of our interviews was carried out over the telephone.

Chapter 6

1   In our study, respondents were invited to share their views on 'teaching excellence' and how it should be measured and evidenced. We recognize that parents are a

diverse group. We cannot claim that the sample (n=24) of parents in the research study on which we draw in this chapter is in any way representative of the diversity of parents with children engaged in undergraduate study at university. While respondents were drawn from different backgrounds in relation to their employment status and their education levels, the majority lived in regions in the north of England (one respondent lived in Northern Ireland), and the majority (n=20) were female. Furthermore, many respondents (n=21) had university-level education themselves, and almost all of them (n=23) were in professional career positions. Notwithstanding the acknowledged limitations of this sample, the data generated some interesting findings of relevance to this chapter, and the discussion of these is illuminated by the literature in the field.

References

Advance HE. (2016), *Frameworks: Essential Frameworks for Enhancing Student Success*. Available online: https://www.heacademy.ac.uk/system/files/downloads/Framework%20for%20Embedding%20Employability%20in%20Higher%20Education_0.pdf (accessed 27 May 2019).

Altbach, P. G., L. Reisberg and H. de Wit (2017), 'Executive Summary', in P. G. Altbach, L. Reisberg and H. de Wit (eds), *Responding to Massification: Differentiation in Postsecondary Education Worldwide* (Global Perspectives on Higher Education book series, vol. 37), xi–xvi, Rotterdam: Sense Publishers.

Annette, J. (2010), 'The Challenge of Developing Civic Engagement in Higher Education in England', *British Journal of Educational Studies*, 58 (4): 451–63.

Appiah, K. A. (2007), *Cosmopolitanism: Ethics in a World of Strangers*, London: Penguin Books.

Arday, J., D. Z. Belluigi and D. Thomas (2021), 'Attempting to Break the Chain: Reimaging Inclusive Pedagogy and Decolonising the Curriculum within the Academy', *Educational Philosophy and Theory*, 53 (3): 298–313.

Arendt, H. (1958), *The Human Condition*, 2nd edn, Chicago: University of Chicago Press.

Arnett, J. J. (2015), *Emerging Adulthood: The Winding Road from the Late Teens through the Twenties*, 2nd edn, New York: Oxford University Press.

Ashwin, P. (2017), 'What Is the Teaching Excellence Framework in the United Kingdom, and Will It Work?' *International Higher Education*, (88): 10–11. https://ejournals.bc.edu/index.php/ihe/article/view/9683/8557

Ashwin, P. (2019), *Knowledge Is Power: The Purpose of Quality Teaching*, WONKHE. Available online: https://wonkhe.com/blogs/knowledge-is-power-the-purpose-of-quality-teaching/ (accessed 22 August 2020).

Ashwin, P. (2020), *Transforming University Education*, London: Bloomsbury.

Bain, K. (2004), *What the Best College Teachers Do*, Cambridge, MA: Harvard University Press.

Bakhtin, M. M. (1986), *Speech Genres and Other Late Essays*, eds C. Emerson and M. Holquist, trans. V. W. McGee, Austin: University of Texas Press.

Ball, S. J. (2013), *Foucault, Power and Education*, Abingdon: Routledge.

Barkas, L. A., J. M. Scott, N. J. Poppitt and P. J. Smith (2019), 'Tinker, Tailor, Policy-Maker: Can the UK Government's Teaching Excellence Framework Deliver Its Objectives?' *Journal of Further and Higher Education*, 43 (6): 801–13.

Barnett, R. (1992), 'Linking Teaching and Research: A Critical Inquiry', *The Journal of Higher Education*, 63 (6): 619–36.

Bartram, B. T. Hathaway and N. Rao (2019), '"Teaching Excellence" in Higher Education: A Comparative Study of English and Australian Academics' Perspectives', *Journal of Further and Higher Education*, 43 (9): 1284–98.

Bayne, S., P. Evans, R. Ewins, J. Knox and J. Lamb (2020), *The Manifesto for Teaching Online*, Cambridge, MA: MIT Press.

Beech, D. (2017), *Going for Gold: Lessons from the TEF Provider Submissions* (Higher Education Policy Institute HEPI Report 99), Oxford: Higher Education Policy Institute.

Bell, A. (2017), 'The Scientific Revolution That Wasn't: The British Society for Social Responsibility in Science', *Radical History Review*, (127): 149–72.

Biesta, G. (2011), 'How Useful Should the University Be?: On the Rise of the Global University and the Crisis in Higher Education', *Qui Parle: Critical Humanities and Social Sciences*, 20 (1): 35–47.

Biesta, G. J. J. (2016), *Good Education in an Age of Measurement*, Abingdon: Routledge.

Biggs, J. and C. Tang (2011), *Teaching for Quality Learning at University*, 4th edn, Maidenhead: Society for Research into Higher Education and Open University Press, McGraw-Hill Education.

Blacker, D. J. (2013), *The Falling Rate of Learning and the Neoliberal Endgame*, Alresford: John Hunt Publishing Ltd.

Blackmore, P. (2016), *Prestige in Academic Life: Excellence and Exclusion*, Abingdon: Routledge.

Blyth, P. and A. Cleminson (2016), *Teaching Excellence Framework: Analysis of Highly Skilled Employment Outcomes*, Department for Education. Available online: https ://assets.publishing.service.gov.uk/government/uploads/system/uploads/attac hment_data/file/557107/Teaching-Excellence-Framework-highly-skilled-em ployment..pdf (accessed 21 July 2020).

Bohm, D. (2004), *On Dialogue*, 2nd edn, Abingdon: Routledge.

Booth, J. (2017), 'The University as a Civic Participant', in J. Wonkhe and S. Martineau (eds), *The Many Faces of the University*, 20–6. Available online: https://wonkhe.com/the-many-faces-of-the-university/ (accessed 17 December 2018).

Bourdieu, P. (1986), 'Forms of Capital', in J. G. Richardson (ed.), *Handbook of Theory and Research for the Sociology of Education*, 241–58, Westport, CT: Greenwood Press.

Bovill, C. (2020), *Co-creating Learning and Teaching: Towards Relational Pedagogy in Higher Education*, St Albans: Critical Publishing.

Boyd, D. C. and F. Singer (2011), 'The Meaning and Evolution of Teaching Excellence: A "radical" Case Study from Radford University, Virginia', in I. Hay (ed.), *Inspiring Academics: Learning with the World's Great University Teachers*, 53–60, Maidenhead: Open University Press/McGraw-Hill Education.

Brink, C. (2018), *The Soul of a University: Why Excellence Is Not Enough*, Bristol: Bristol University Press.

Brinkmann, S. and T. McTurk (2017), *Stand Firm: Resisting the Self-Improvement Craze*, Cambridge: Polity Press.

British Society for Social Responsibility in Science (BSSRS) (2009), 'Beginnings'. Available online: http://www.bssrs.org/in-the-news (accessed 23 August 2019).

Brockbank, A. and I. McGill (2007), *Facilitating Reflective Learning in Higher Education*, 2nd edn, Maidenhead: Society for Research into Higher Education and Open University Press/McGraw-Hill Education.

Brookfield, S. D. (1995), *Becoming a Critically Reflective Teacher*, San Francisco, CA: Jossey-Bass.

Brooks, R. (2004), '"My Mum Would Be As Pleased As Punch If I Actually Went, But My Dad Seems A Bit More Particular About It": Parental Involvement In Young People's Higher Education Choices', *British Educational Research Journal*, 30 (4): 495–514.

Brown, P., H. Lauder and D. Ashton (2008), 'Education, Globalisation and the Future of the Knowledge Economy', *European Educational Research Journal*, 7 (2): 131–56. Available online https://journals.sagepub.com/doi/pdf/10.2304/eerj.2008.7.2.131 (accessed 6 May 2021).

Brown, P., H. Lauder and D. Ashton (2012), *The Global Auction: The Broken Promises of Education, Jobs, and Incomes*, Oxford: Oxford University Press.

Bryman, A. (2008), *Social Research Methods*, 3rd edn, Oxford: Oxford University Press.

Bunce, L. (2019), 'The Voice of the Student as a "Consumer"', in S. Lygo-Baker, I. M. Kinchin and N. Winstone (eds), *Engaging Student Voices in Higher Education: Diverse Perspectives and Expectations in Partnership*, 55–70, London: Palgrave Macmillan.

Bunce, L., A. Baird and S. E. Jones (2017), 'The Student-As-Consumer Approach In Higher Education And Its Effects on Academic Performance', *Studies in Higher Education*, 42 (11): 1958–78.

Burns, D., N. Dagnall and M. Holt (2020), 'Assessing the Impact of the COVID-19 Pandemic on Student Wellbeing at Universities in the United Kingdom: A Conceptual Analysis', *Frontiers in Education*, 5: 1–10. Available online: from https://www.frontiersin.org/articles/10.3389/feduc.2020.582882/full (accessed 1 February 2021).

Carasso, H. and W. Locke (2016), 'Paying the Price of Expansion: Why More for Undergraduates in England Means Less for Everyone', in P. John and J. Fanghanel (eds), *Dimensions of Marketisation in Higher Education*, 26–37, Abingdon: Routledge.

Carr, W. and A. Hartnett (1996), *Education and the Struggle for Democracy: The Politics of Educational Ideas*, Buckingham: Open University Press.

Chen, Yi. (2017), *Practising Rhythmanalysis. Theories and Methodologies*, London: Rowman & Littlefield International, Ltd.

Clegg, S. (2007), 'The Demotic Turn – Excellence By Fiat', in A. Skelton (ed.), *International Perspectives on Teaching Excellence in Higher Education: Improving Knowledge and Practice*, 91–102, Abingdon: Routledge.

Cole, D. and M. Tibby (2013), *Defining and Developing Your Approach to Employability: A Framework for Higher Education Institutions*, York: The Higher Education Academy.

Coles, M. I. and B. Gent, eds (2020), *Education for Survival: The Pedagogy of Compassion*, Stoke-on-Trent: Trentham Books.

Collini, S. (2012), *What Are Universities For?* London: Penguin.

Collini, S. (2017), *Speaking of Universities*, London: Verso.

Consortium of students' unions (2017), *Teaching Excellence: The Student Perspective*. Available online: https://wonkhe.com/wp-content/wonkhe-uploads/2017/11/tef-pr-research-report-2.pdf (accessed 9 January 2020).

Cook-Sather, A. (2020), 'Respecting Voices: How The Co-Creation of Teaching and Learning Can Support Academic Staff, Underrepresented Students, and Equitable Practices', *Higher Education*, 79 (5): 885–901.

Cook-Sather, A. and C. Des-Ogugua (2019), 'Lessons We Still Need to Learn on Creating More Inclusive and Responsive Classrooms: Recommendations from One Student–Faculty Partnership Programme', *International Journal of Inclusive Education*, 23 (6): 594–608.

Cooper, T. (2019), 'Rethinking Teaching Excellence in Australian Higher Education', *International Journal of Comparative Education and Development*, 21 (2): 83–98.

Creswell, J. W. (2007), *Qualitative Inquiry and Research Design: Choosing Among Five Approaches*, 2nd edn, London: Sage.

Cruickshank, J. (2016), 'Putting Business at the Heart of Higher Education: On Neoliberal Interventionism and Audit Culture in UK Universities', *Open Library of Humanities*, 2 (1): e3, 1–33.

Darby, F. and J. M. Lang (2019), *Small Teaching Online: Applying Learning Science in Online Classes*, San Francisco, CA: Jossey Bass.

Davies, M. and R. Barnett (2015), 'Introduction', in M. Davies and R. Barnett (eds), *The Palgrave Handbook of Critical Thinking in Higher Education*, 1–25, London: Palgrave MacMillan.

Dawson, C. (2007), *A Practical Guide to Research Methods: A User-Friendly Manual for Mastering Research Techniques and Projects*, 3rd edn, Oxford: How To Books.

Department for Business, Energy & Industrial Strategy (2017), *Industrial Strategy: Building A Britain Fit for the Future*. Available online: https://assets.publishing.service.gov.uk/government/uploads/system/uploads/attachment_data/file/664563/industrial-strategy-white-paper-web-ready-version.pdf (accessed 21 August 2018).

Department for Business, Innovation and Skills (2011), *Higher Education: Students at the Heart of the System*, Cm 8122. Available online: https://assets.publishing.service.gov.uk/government/uploads/system/uploads/attachment_data/file/31384/11-944-higher-education-students-at-heart-of-system.pdf (accessed 23 June 2019).

Department for Business, Innovation and Skills (2016), *Success as a Knowledge Economy: Teaching Excellence, Social Mobility and Student Choice*, Cm 9258. Available online: https://www.gov.uk/government/publications/higher-education-success-as-a-knowledge-economy-white-paper (accessed 25 May 2016).

Department for Education (2017), *Teaching Excellence and Student Outcomes Framework Specification*. Available online: https://webarchive.nationalarchives.gov.uk/20180104232246/https://www.gov.uk/government/publications/teaching-excellence-and-student-outcomes-framework-specification (accessed 23 June 2019).

Dixon, F. J. and R. Pilkington (2017), 'Poor Relations? Tensions and Torment: A View Of Excellence in Teaching and Learning from the Cinderella Sector', *Teaching in Higher Education*, 22 (4): 437–50.

Dollinger, M. and L. Mercer-Mapstone (2019), 'What's in a Name? Unpacking Students' Roles in Higher Education through Neoliberal and Social Justice Lenses', *Teaching and Learning Inquiry*, 7 (2): 73–89.

Elden, S. (2004), *Understanding Henri Lefebvre: Theory and the Possible*, London: Continuum.

Elias, A., J. Ben, F. Mansouri and Y. Paradies (2021), 'Racism and Nationalism during and beyond the COVID-19 Pandemic', *Ethnic and Racial Studies*, 44 (5): 783–93.

English, F. W. and C. L. Bolton (2016), *Bourdieu for Educators: Policy and Practice*, London: Sage.

Eringfeld, S. (2021), 'Higher Education and Its Post-Coronial Future: Utopian Hopes and Dystopian Fears at Cambridge University during Covid-19', *Studies in Higher Education*, 46 (1): 146–57.

Felten, P. and L. M. Lambert (2020), *Relationship-Rich Education: How Human Connections Drive Success in College*, Baltimore, MD: Johns Hopkins University Press.

Field, J. (2017), *Social Capital*, 3rd edn, Abingdon: Routledge.

Ford, M. (2016), *The Rise of the Robots: Technology and the Threat of Mass Unemployment*, London: Oneworld.

Forde, C., M. McMahon, A. D. McPhee and F. Patrick (2006), *Professional Development, Reflection and Enquiry*, London: Paul Chapman Publishing.

Forrester, G. and D. Garratt (2016), *Education Policy Unravelled*, 2nd edn, London: Bloomsbury.

Freeman, R. E. (2010), *Strategic Management: A Stakeholder Approach*, Cambridge: Cambridge University Press.

French, A. (2017), 'Contextualising Excellence in Higher Education Teaching: Understanding the Policy Landscape', in A. French and M. O'Leary (eds), *Teaching Excellence in Higher Education: Challenges, Changes and the Teaching Excellence Framework*, 5–38, Bingley: Emerald Publishing Limited.

French, A. and K. C. Thomas, eds (2020), *Challenging the Teaching Excellence Framework: Diversity Deficits in Higher Education Evaluations*, Bingley: Emerald Publishing.

Fullan, M. and A. Hargreaves (1996), *What's Worth Fighting For in Your School?* New York: Teachers College Press.

Garven, F., J. McLean and l. Pattoni (2016), *Asset-Based Approaches: Their Rise, Role and Reality*, Edinburgh and London: Dunedin Academic Press Ltd.

George, E. S. (2006), 'Positioning Higher Education for the Knowledge Based Economy', *Higher Education*, 52 (4): 589–610.

Georgiadou, E., H. Rahanu, K. Siakas, C. McGuinness, J. A. Edwards, V. Hill, N. Khan, P. Kirby, J. Cavanagh and R. Knezevic (2018), 'Fake News and Critical Thinking in Information Evaluation', Bihac, Bosnia and Herzegovina, Western Balkan Information Literacy Conference WBILC 2018. Available online: https://www.researchgate.net/publication/325930497_Fake_News_and_Critical_Thinking_in_Information_Evaluation (accessed 2 March 2021).

Gibbons, S. and A. Vignoles (2012), 'Geography, Choice and Participation in Higher Education in England', *Regional Science and Urban Economics*, 42 (1): 98–113.

Gibbs, G. (2010), *Dimensions of Quality*, York: Higher Education Academy.

Gibbs, G. (2012), *Implications of 'Dimensions of Quality' in a Market Environment*, York: Higher Education Academy.

Goddard, J., E. Hazelkorn, L. Kempton and P. Vallance (2016), 'Introduction: Why the Civic University?', in J. Goddard, E. Hazelkorn, L. Kempton and P. Vallance (eds), *The Civic University: The Policy and Leadership Challenges*, 3–15, Cheltenham: Edward Elgar Publishing.

Goedegebuure, L. and L. Meek (2021), 'Crisis – What Crisis?', *Studies in Higher Education*, 46 (1): 1–4.

Gottdiener, M. (1993), 'A Marx for Our Time: Henri Lefebvre and the Production of Space', *Sociological Theory*, 11 (1):129–34.

Gourlay, L. and J. Stevenson (2017), 'Teaching Excellence in Higher Education: Critical Perspectives', *Teaching in Higher Education*, 22 (4): 391–5.

Gregory, M., ed. (2013), *Teaching Excellence in Higher Education*, London: Palgrave MacMillan.

Gregory, S. (2010), 'Collaborative Approaches: Putting Colour in a Grey Area', *International Journal of Community Music*, 3 (3): 387–97.

Grey, D. and C. Osborne (2020), 'Perceptions and Principles of Personal Tutoring', *Journal of Further and Higher Education*, 44 (3): 285–99.

Gunn, V. and A. Fisk (2013), *Considering Teaching Excellence in Higher Education: 2007-2013: A Literature Review since the CHERI Report 2007*, York: Higher Education Academy.

Hanken, I. M. (2016), 'Peer Learning in Specialist Higher Music Education', *Arts & Humanities in Higher Education*, 15 (3–4): 364–75.

Harper, S. R. and S. J. Quaye (2009), 'Beyond Sameness, with Engagement and Outcomes for All: An Introduction', in S. R. Harper and S. J. Quaye (eds), *Student Engagement in Higher Education: Theoretical Perspectives and Practical Approaches for Diverse Populations*, 1–15, Abingdon: Routledge.

Harvey, D. (1991), 'Afterword', in H. Lefebvre, *The Production of Space*, trans. D. Nicholson-Smith, Oxford: Blackwell.

Hay, I., ed. (2011a), *Inspiring Academics: Learning with the World's Great University Teachers*, Maidenhead: Open University Press/McGraw-Hill Education.

Hay, I. (2011b), 'From Fear to Flourish', in I. Hay (ed.), *Inspiring Academics: Learning with the World's Great University Teachers*, 208–12, Maidenhead: Open University Press/McGraw-Hill Education.

Hayes, S. (2019), *The Labour of Words in Higher Education: Is It Time to Reoccupy Policy?* Leiden: Brill.

Hazelkorn, E. (2015), *Rankings and the Reshaping of Higher Education: The Battle for World-Class Excellence*, 2nd edn, London: Palgrave Macmillan.

Healey, M. (2011), 'Excellence and Scholarship in Teaching: Some Reflections', in I. Hay (ed.), *Inspiring Academics: Learning with the World's Great University Teachers*, 198–207, Maidenhead: Open University Press and McGraw-Hill Education.

Healey, M., A. Flint and K. Harrington (2016), 'Students as Partners: Reflections on a Conceptual Model', *Teaching and Learning Inquiry*, 4 (2): 1–13.

Heath, S. and E. Calvert (2013), 'Gifts, Loans and Intergenerational Support for Young Adults', *Sociology*, 47 (6): 1120–35.

Held, D. (2010), *Cosmopolitanism: Ideas and Realities*, Cambridge: Polity Press.

Higher Education Funding Council for England (HEFCE) (2017), *About the TEF*. Available online: https://webarchive.nationalarchives.gov.uk/20170712122815/http://www.hefce.ac.uk/lt/tef/whatistef/ (accessed 23 June 2019).

Hockings, C. (2010), *Inclusive Learning and Teaching in Higher Education: A Synthesis of Research*. Available online: https://www.advance-he.ac.uk/knowledge-hub/inclusive-learning-and-teaching-higher-education-synthesis-research (accessed 5 January 2021).

Ingold, T. (2018), *Anthropology And/As Education*, Abingdon: Routledge.

James, N. and H. Busher (2009), *Online Interviewing*, London: Sage.

Jensen, K., J. Adams and K. Strickland (2014), 'Inspirational Teaching: Beyond Excellence and Towards Collaboration for Learning with Sustained Impact', *Journal of Perspectives in Applied Academic Practice*, 2 (2): 37–41.

Johnston, T. C. (2010), 'Who and What Influences Choice of University? Student and University Perceptions', *American Journal of Business Education*, 3 (10): 15–24.

Joint Information Systems Committee (JISC) (2014), *Developing Digital Literacies*. Available online: https://www.jisc.ac.uk/guides/developing-digital-literacies (accessed 25 January 2021).

Jung, J. (2015), *The Concept of Care in Curriculum Studies: Juxtaposing Currere and Hakbeolism*, Abingdon: Routledge.

Kandiko, C. B. and M. Mawer (2013), *Student Expectations and Perceptions of Higher Education*, London: King's Learning Institute.

Keep, E. (2020), *COVID-19 – Potential Consequences for Education, Training, and Skills* (SKOPE Issues Paper 36). Available online: https://skope.ox.ac.uk/wp-content/uploads/2020/07/SKOPE-Issues-Paper-36-.-E.-Keep.-Covid-19.pdf (accessed 27 January 2021).

Kemp-King, S. (2016), *The Graduate Premium: Manna, Myth or Plain Mis-Selling?* London: The Intergenerational Foundation.

Kempton, L. (2016), 'Institutional Challenges and Tensions', in J. Goddard, E. Hazelkorn, L. Kempton and P. Vallance (eds), *The Civic University: The Policy and Leadership Challenges*, 281–97, Cheltenham: Edward Elgar Publishing.

Knight, P. and M. Yorke (2004), *Learning, Curriculum and Employability in Higher Education*, Abingdon: Routledge Falmer.

Kupfer, A. (2011), 'Towards a Theoretical Framework for the Comparative Understanding of Globalisation, Higher Education, the Labour Market and Inequality', *Journal of Education and Work*, 24 (1–2): 185–208.

Lauder, H., M. Young, H. Daniels, M. Balarin and J. Lowe (2012), 'Introduction: Educating for the Knowledge Economy? Critical Perspectives', in H. Lauder, M. Young, H. Daniels, M. Balarin and J. Lowe (eds), *Educating for the Knowledge Economy? Critical Perspectives*, 1–24, Abingdon: Routledge.

Lawrie, G., E. Marquis, E. Fuller, T. Newman, M. Qui, M. Nomikoudis, F. Roelofs and L. van Dam (2017), 'Moving towards Inclusive Learning and Teaching: A Synthesis of Recent Literature', *Teaching & Learning Inquiry*, 5 (1): 1–13.

Lefebvre, H. ([1974] 1991), trans. D. Nicholson-Smith, *The Production of Space*, Oxford: Blackwell.

Lefebvre, H. ([1992] 2004), trans. Elden, S. and G. Moore, *Rhythmanalysis: Space, Time and Everyday Life*, London: Continuum.

Lefebvre, H. (2014, 2002), *The Critique of Everyday Life: The One-Volume Edition*, Volume 2: Foundations for a Sociology of the Everyday, London: Verso.

Lefebvre, H. and C. Régulier ([1985] 2004), [originally published as 'Le projet rythmanalytique', *Communications*, 41 (1985): 191–9.] in *The Rhythmanalytical Project* in H. Lefebvre ([1992] 2004), trans. S. Elden, and G. Moore, *Rhythmanalysis: Space, Time and Everyday Life*, London: Continuum.

Legge, K. (1995), *Human Resource Management: Rhetorics and Realities*, Basingstoke: MacMillan Press.

Levine, F. J., N. S. Nasir, C. Rios-Aguilar, R. E. Gildersleeve, K. J. Rosich, M. Bang, N. E. Bell, and M. A. Holsapple (2021), *Voices from the Field: The Impact of COVID-19 on Early Career Scholars and Doctoral Students* [Focus group study report]. American Educational Research Association and Spencer Foundation. Available online: https://doi.org/10.3102/aera20211 (accessed 4 February 2021).

Lewis, J. and A. West (2017), 'Intergenerational Relations between English Students, Graduates Living at Home, and their Parents', *Social Policy and Administration*, 51 (7): 1248–66.

Lewis, J., A. West, J. Roberts and P. Noden (2015), 'Parents' Involvement and University Students' Independence', *Families, Relationships and Societies*, 4 (3): 417–32.

Light, G., R. Cox and S. Calkins (2009), *Learning and Teaching in Higher Education: The Reflective Professional*, 2nd edn, London: Sage.

Little, B. (2005), 'Policies Towards More Work-Focused Higher Education – Are They Meeting Employers' Needs?' *Tertiary Education and Management*, 11 (2): 131–46.

Little, B., W. Locke, J. Parker and J. Richardson (2007), *Excellence in Teaching and Learning: A Review of the Literature for the Higher Education Academy*, York: Higher Education Academy.

Lowden, K., S. Hall, D. Elliot and J. Lewin (2011), *Employers' Perceptions of the Employability Skills of New Graduates*, London: Edge Foundation. Available online: https://www.educationandemployers.org/wp-content/uploads/2014/06/employability_skills_as_pdf_-_final_online_version.pdf (accessed 27 May 2019).

Lubicz-Nawrocka, T. and K. Bunting (2019), 'Student Perceptions of Teaching Excellence: An Analysis of Student-Led Teaching Award Nomination Data', *Teaching in Higher Education*, 24 (1): 63–80.

Lygo-Baker, S., I. M. Kinchin and N. Winstone, eds (2019), *Engaging Student Voices in Higher Education: Diverse Perspectives and Expectations in Partnership*, London: Palgrave Macmillan.

Maguire, D., L. Dale and M. Pauli (2020), *Learning and Teaching Reimagined: A New Dawn for Higher Education?* Available online: https://www.jisc.ac.uk/reports/learning-and-teaching-reimagined-a-new-dawn-for-higher-education# (accessed 25 January 2021).

Maisuria, A. and S. Helmes (2019), *Life for the Academic in the Neoliberal University*, Abingdon: Routledge.

Marginson, S. (2018), 'Global Trends in Higher Education Financing: The United Kingdom', *International Journal of Educational Development*, 58: 26–36.

Mason, J. (2002), *Qualitative Researching*, 2nd edn, London: Sage.

Mason, P. (2016), *PostCapitalism: A Guide to Our Future*, London: Penguin Books.

Mathers, H. (2005), *Steel City Scholars: The Centenary History of the University of Sheffield*, London: James and James.

McCowan, T. (2015), 'Should Universities Promote Employability?' *Theory and Research in Education*, 13 (3): 267–85.

McFarlane, K. J. (2016), 'Tutoring the Tutors: Supporting Effective Personal Tutoring', *Active Learning in Higher Education*, 17 (1): 77–88.

McKenzie, L. and C. Schofield (2018), 'Degrees of Freedom: College-Based Higher Education Students' Choices and Views on the Top-Up Mode of Higher Education', *Research in Post-Compulsory Education*, 23 (3): 314–27.

Mercer-Mapstone, L., M. Islam and T. Reid (2021), 'Are We Just Engaging 'The Usual Suspects'? Challenges in and Practical Strategies for Supporting Equity and Diversity in Student-Staff Partnership Initiatives', *Teaching in Higher Education*, 26 (2): 227–45.

Middleton, S. (2017), 'Henri Lefebvre on Education: Critique and Pedagogy', *Policy Futures in Education*, 15 (4): 410–26.

Middleton, S. (2014), *Henri Lefebvre and Education: Space, History, Theory*, Abingdon: Routledge.

Miller, P. B. W. and P. R. Bahnson (2010), 'The Spirit of Accounting: Mencken was Right and So Were We', *Accounting Today*, 24 (9): 16–17.

Mimirinis, M. (2020), 'What do Undergraduate Students Understand By Excellent Teaching?' *Higher Education Research & Development*. DOI: 10.1080/07294360.2020.1847048

Minocha, S., D. Hristov and S. Leahy-Harland (2018), 'Developing a Future-Ready Global Workforce: A Case Study from a Leading UK University', *The International Journal of Management Education*, 16 (2): 245–55.

Moore, R. (2021), 'The Free-Market Gamble: Has Covid Broken UK Universities?' *The Observer*. Available online: https://www.theguardian.com/education/2021/jan/17/free-market-gamble-has-covid-broken-uk-universities (accessed 20 January 2021).

Morley, L. (2003), *Quality and Power in Higher Education*, Maidenhead: Society for Research into Higher Education and Open University Press.

Naidoo, R., A. Shankar and E. Veer (2011), 'The Consumerist Turn in Higher Education: Policy Aspirations and Outcomes', *Journal of Marketing Management*, 27 (11–12): 1142–62.

Nebres, B. F. (2017), 'Political Extremes in the Philippines: Academic Leadership and Social Engagement', in F. Su and M. Wood (eds), *Cosmopolitan Perspectives on Academic Leadership in Higher Education*, 75–90, London: Bloomsbury.

Nixon, J. (2012), *Higher Education and the Public Good: Imagining the University*, London: Continuum.

Nixon, J. (2008), *Towards the Virtuous University: The Moral Bases of Academic Practice*, Abingdon: Routledge.

Nixon, J. (2007), 'Excellence and the Good Society', in A. Skelton (ed.), *International Perspectives on Teaching Excellence in Higher Education: Improving Knowledge and Practice*, 15–31, Abingdon: Routledge.

Norton, L. (2016), 'Developing Criticality in Learning and Teaching through Pedagogical Action Research', in P. John and J. Fanghanel (eds), *Dimensions of Marketisation in Higher Education*, 154–63, Abingdon: Routledge.

O'Brien, E. (2020), *Start the Week* with Andrew Marr, Episode: James Joyce, 15 June, BBC Radio 4. Available online:https://www.bbc.co.uk/programmes/b006r9xr/episodes/player (accessed 2 July 2020).

O'Connor, S. (2013), 'Graduate Data Reveal England's Lost and Indebted Generation', *Financial Times*, 18 November. Available online: https://www.ft.com/content/ed70d986-5048-11e3-9f0d-00144feabdc0 (accessed 7 August 2018).

Office for Students (n.d.), *Teaching Excellence and Student Outcomes Framework*. Available online: https://www.officeforstudents.org.uk/for-students/the-tef/ (accessed 13 August 2019).

Office for Students (2019), *The Teaching Excellence and Student Outcomes Framework (TEF): A Short Guide to the Awards*. Available online: https://www.officeforstudents.org.uk/media/0c6bd23e-57b8-4f22-a236-fb27346cde6e/tef_short_guide_-june_2019_final.pdf (accessed 19 August 2019).

Office for Students (2020a), *English Higher Education 2020*. The Office for Students Annual Review. Available online: https://www.officeforstudents.org.uk/media/bd2b038b-126a-4ad1-a4fe-a4bc30414972/2020-ofs-annual-review-web-accessible.pdf (accessed 22 February 2021).

Office for Students (2020b), *'Digital Poverty' Risks Leaving Students Behind*. Available online: https://www.officeforstudents.org.uk/news-blog-and-events/press-and-media/digital-poverty-risks-leaving-students-behind/ (accessed 25 January 2021).

Okupe, A. and E. Medland (2019), 'Pluralising "Student Voices": Evaluating Teaching Practice', in S. Lygo-Baker, I. M. Kinchin and N. Winstone (eds), *Engaging Student Voices in Higher Education: Diverse Perspectives and Expectations in Partnership*, 261–77, London: Palgrave Macmillan.

O'Leary, M., V. Cui and A. French (2019), *Understanding, Recognising and Rewarding Teaching Quality in Higher Education: An Exploration of the Impact and Implications of the Teaching Excellence Framework*, Project Report for UCU. Available online: http://www.ucu.org.uk/media/10092/Impact-of-TEF-report-Feb-2019/pdf/ImpactofTEFreportFEb2019 (accessed 17 April 2019).

O'Leary, M. and P. Wood (2019), 'Reimagining Teaching Excellence: Why Collaboration, Rather than Competition, Holds the Key to Improving Teaching and Learning in Higher Education', *Educational Review*, 71 (1): 122–39.

O'Leary, S. (2017), 'Graduates' Experiences of, and Attitudes towards, the Inclusion of Employability-Related Support in Undergraduate Degree Programmes: Trends and Variations by Subject Discipline and Gender', *Journal of Education and Work*, 30 (1): 84–105.

Olssen, M. (2010), *Liberalism, Neoliberalism, Social Democracy: Thin Communitarian Perspectives on Political Philosophy and Education*, Abingdon: Routledge.

Olssen, M., J. Codd and A. M. O'Neill (2004), *Education Policy, Globalization, Citizenship and Democracy*, London: Sage.

Palmer, P. (1993), *To Know As We Are Known: Education as a Spiritual Journey*, New York: HarperCollins.

Palmer, P. (2017), *The Courage to Teach: Exploring the Inner Landscape of a Teacher's Life*, 20th edn, San Francisco, CA: Jossey-Bass.

Perez, K. (2016), 'Striving Toward a Space for Equity and Inclusion in Physics Classrooms', *Teaching and Learning Together in Higher Education*, 18: 1–5.

Peters, M. (2004), 'Higher Education, Globalization and the Knowledge Economy', in M. Walker and J. Nixon (eds), *Reclaiming Universities from a Runaway World*, 67–82, Maidenhead: The Society for Research into Higher Education and Open University Press/McGraw-Hill Education.

Public Health England (2020), *Beyond the Data: Understanding the Impact of COVID-19 on BAME Groups*. Available online: https://assets.publishing.service.gov.uk/government/uploads/system/uploads/attachment_data/file/892376/COVID_stakeholder_engagement_synthesis_beyond_the_data.pdf (accessed 20 January 2021).

Putnam, R. D. (2001), *Bowling Alone: The Collapse and Revival of American Community*, New York: Touchstone/Simon and Schuster.

Quality Assurance Agency for Higher Education (2015), *Characteristics Statement: Foundation Degree (UK Quality Code for Higher Education Part A: Setting and maintaining academic standards)*. Available online: https://www.qaa.ac.uk/docs/qaa/quality-code/foundation-degree-characteristics-15.pdf?sfvrsn=ea05f781_10 (accessed 17 July 2019).

Race, P. (2005), *Making Learning Happen: A Guide for Post-Compulsory Education*, London: Sage.

Race, P. and R. Pickford (2007), *Making Teaching Work: 'Teaching Smarter' in Post-Compulsory Education*, London: Sage.

Ramsden, P. (2003), *Learning to Teach in Higher Education*, 2nd edn, Abingdon: Routledge.

Ranson, S. and J. Stewart (1994), *Management for the Public Domain: Enabling the Learning Society*, Basingstoke: Macmillan.

Readings, B. (1996), *The University in Ruins*, Cambridge, MA: Harvard University Press.

Richardson, T. (2011), 'A Schizocartography of a Redbrick', *Spaces & Flows: An International Journal of Urban & Extra Urban Studies*, 1 (1): 119–27.

Roberts, P. (2015), *The Impulse Society: What's Wrong With Getting What We Want?* London: Bloomsbury.

Robertson, A., E. Cleaver and F. Smart (2019), *Beyond the Metrics: Identifying, Evidencing and Enhancing the Less Tangible Assets of Higher Education*, QAA Scotland. https://www.enhancementthemes.ac.uk/docs/ethemes/evidence-for-enhancement/beyond-the-metrics-identifying-evidencing-and-enhancing-the-less-tangible-assets-of-higher-education.pdf?sfvrsn=ca37c681_8 (accessed 6 May 2021).

Robson, S. (2017), 'Developing and Supporting Teaching Excellence in Higher Education', in A. French and M. O'Leary (eds), *Teaching Excellence in Higher Education: Challenges, Changes and the Teaching Excellence Framework*, 109–36, Bingley: Emerald Publishing.

Rowland, S. (2008), 'Collegiality and Intellectual Love', *British Journal of Sociology of Education*, 29 (3): 353–60.

Runté, M. and R. Runté (2018), 'Excellence for What? Policy Development and the Discourse on the Purpose of Higher Education', in C. Broughan, G. Steventon and L. Clouder (eds), *Global Perspectives on Teaching Excellence: A New Era for Higher Education*, 66–80, Abingdon: Routledge.

Sachs, J. (2004), 'Sitting Uneasily at the Table', in M. Walker and J. Nixon (eds), *Reclaiming Universities from a Runaway World*, 100–13, Maidenhead: Open University Press/McGraw-Hill Education.

Said, E. W. (1994), *Culture and Imperialism*, London: Vintage.

Saunders, D. B. and G. B. Ramírez (2017), 'Against "Teaching Excellence": Ideology, Commodification, and Enabling the Neoliberalization of Postsecondary Education', *Teaching in Higher Education*, 22 (4): 396–407.

Saunders, V. and K. Zuzel (2010), 'Evaluating Employability Skills: Employer and Student Perceptions', *Bioscience Education*, 15 (1): 1–15.

Schoper, S. E. and E. C. Amelse (2020), 'A New Narrative About Emotions and Their Connection to Learning', in L. Parson and C. C. Ozaki (eds), *Teaching and Learning for Social Justice and Equity in Higher Education*, 179–97, London: Palgrave Macmillan.

Scott, P. (2016), 'Private Commodities and Public Goods: Markets and Values in Higher Education', in P. John and J. Fanghanel (eds), *Dimensions of Marketisation in Higher Education*, 15–25, Abingdon: Routledge.

Seale, J., S. Gibson, J. Haynes and A. Potter (2015), 'Power and Resistance: Reflections on the Rhetoric and Reality of Using Participatory Methods to Promote Student Voice and Engagement in Higher Education', *Journal of Further and Higher Education*, 39 (4): 534–52.

Shields, R. (2004), 'Henri Lefebvre' in P. Hubbard, R. Kitchin and G. Valentine (eds), *Key Thinkers on Space and Place*, 208–13, London: Sage.

Shumar, W. (1997), *College for Sale: A Critique of the Commodification of Higher Education*, London: Falmer Press.

Silver, H. (1999), 'The Universities' Speaking Conscience: "Bruce Truscot" and Redbrick University', *History of Education*, 28 (2): 173–89.

Skelton, A. (2005), *Understanding Teaching Excellence in Higher Education: Towards a Critical Approach*, Abingdon: Routledge.

Skelton, A., ed. (2007), *International Perspectives on Teaching Excellence in Higher Education: Improving Knowledge and Practice*, Abingdon: Routledge.

Slane, R. (2017), *Teaching Excellence Framework: Bridging the Gap between Employability & Employment — Part 1*. Available online: https://www.economicmodelling.co.uk/2017/04/28/teaching-excellence-framework-bridging-gap-employability-employment-part-1/ (accessed 16 June 2020).

Smyth, J. (2017), *The Toxic University: Zombie Leadership, Academic Rock Stars and Neoliberal Ideology*, London: Palgrave Macmillan.

Stewart, C., A. Wall and S. Marciniec (2016), 'Mixed Signals: Do College Graduates Have the Soft Skills That Employers Want?' *Competition Forum*, 14 (2): 276–81.

Støren, L. A. and P. O. Aamodt (2010), 'The Quality of Higher Education and Employability of Graduates', *Quality in Higher Education*, 16 (3): 297–313.

Su, F. and C. Beaumont (2010), 'Evaluating the Use of a Wiki for Collaborative Learning', *Innovations in Education and Teaching International*, 47 (4): 417–31.

Su, F. and M. Wood (2012), 'What Makes a Good University Lecturer? Students' Perceptions of Teaching Excellence', *Journal of Applied Research in Higher Education*, 4 (2): 142–55.

Su, F. and M. Wood (2017), 'Towards an "Ordinary" Cosmopolitanism in Everyday Academic Practice in Higher Education', *Journal of Educational Administration and History*, 49 (1): 22–36.

The Intergenerational Commission (2018), *A New Generational Contract: The Final Report of the Intergenerational Commission*. Available online: https://www.resolutionfoundation.org/app/uploads/2018/05/A-New-Generational-Contract-Full-PDF.pdf (accessed 13 May 2018).

The Robbins Report (1963), *Higher Education: Report of the Committee Appointed by the Prime Minister under the Chairmanship of Lord Robbins*, London: Her Majesty's Stationery Office. Available online: http://www.educationengland.org.uk/documents/robbins/robbins1963.html#02 (accessed 11 June 2018).

Thiel, J. (2019), 'The UK National Student Survey: An Amalgam of Discipline and Neo-Liberal Governmentality', *British Educational Research Journal*, 45 (3): 538–53.

Thomas, L. (2006), 'Widening Participation and the Increased Need for Personal Tutoring', in P. Hixenbaugh, L. Thomas and S. Barfield (eds), *Personal Tutoring in Higher Education*, 21–31, Stoke on Trent: Trentham Books.

Thompson, D. W. (2017), 'How Valuable Is "Short Project" Placement Experience to Higher Education Students?' *Journal of Further and Higher Education*, 41 (3): 413–24.

Tierney, W. G. (2016), 'Portrait of Higher Education in the Twenty-First Century: John Henry Newman's "The Idea of a University"', *International Journal of Leadership in Education*, 19 (1): 5–16.

Tight, M. (2019), 'Mass Higher Education and Massification', *Higher Education Policy*, 32: 93–108.

Tilak, J. B. G. (2008), 'Transition from Higher Education As a Public Good to Higher Education As a Private Good: The Saga of Indian experience', *Journal of Asian Public Policy*, 1 (2): 220–34.

Tomlinson, S. (2005), *Education in a Post-Welfare Society*, 2nd edn, Maidenhead: Open University Press.

Tressler, R. and R. Piper (2017), *Taking the Strategic Approach to Supporting Students' Mental Health*. Available online: https://wonkhe.com/blogs/analysis-strategic-approach-to-supporting-students-mental-health/ (accessed 25 June 2018).

Trowler, V. (2010), *Student Engagement Literature Review*, York: Higher Education Academy. Available online: https://www.heacademy.ac.uk/system/files/StudentEngagementLiteratureReview:1.pdf (accessed 30 November 2019).

Tsvetkova, E. and S. Lomer (2019), 'Academic Excellence As "Competitiveness Enhancement" in Russian Higher Education', *International Journal of Comparative Education and Development*, 21 (2): 127–44.

Turner, F. M. (1996), 'Newman's University and Ours', in F. M. Turner and J. H. Newman (eds), *The Idea of a University*, 282–301, New Haven, CT: Yale University Press.

Universities and Colleges Admissions Service (UCAS) (n.d.), *Is conservatoire Study Right for Me?* Available online: https://www.ucas.com/conservatoires/conservatoire-study-right-me (accessed 5 January 2020).

Vallance, P. (2016), 'The Historical Roots and Development of the Civic University', in J. Goddard, E. Hazelkorn, L. Kempton and P. Vallance (eds), *The Civic University: The Policy and Leadership Challenges*, 16–33, Cheltenham: Edward Elgar Publishing Limited.

Von Bergen, C. W. and M. S. Bressler (2017), 'The Counterproductive Effects of Helicopter Universities', *Research in Higher Education Journal*, 33: 1–17.

Ward, S. and C. Eden (2009), *Key Issues in Education Policy*, London: Sage.

Warner, M. (2002), *Publics and Counterpublics*, New York: Zone Books.

Wellington, J. (2000), *Educational Research: Contemporary Issues and Practical Approaches*, London: Continuum.

West, A., J. Roberts, J. Lewis and P. Noden (2015), 'Paying for Higher Education in England: Funding Policy and Families', *British Journal of Educational Studies*, 63 (1): 23–45.

Wheeler, S. and J. Birtle (1993), *A Handbook for Personal Tutors*, Buckingham: SRHE and Open University Press.

Whitty, G. (2002), *Making Sense of Education Policy*, London: Paul Chapman Publishing.

Wilde, O. (1980), *Lady Windermere's Fan: A Play about a Good Woman*, London: Ernest Benn.

Williams, G. (2016), 'Reflections on Evidence and Higher Education Policy', in P. John and J. Fanghanel (eds), *Dimensions of Marketisation in Higher Education*, 201–9, Abingdon: Routledge.

Wood, M. and F. Su (2017), 'What Makes an Excellent Lecturer? Academics' Perspectives on the Discourse of "Teaching Excellence" in Higher Education', *Teaching in Higher Education*, 22 (4): 451–66.

Wood, M. and F. Su (2019), 'Parents as "Stakeholders" and their Conceptions of Teaching Excellence in Higher Education in England', *International Journal of Comparative Education and Development*, 21 (2): 99–111.

Wood, P. (2017), 'From Teaching Excellence to Emergent Pedagogies: A Complex Process Alternative to Understanding the Role of Teaching in Higher Education', in A. French and M. O'Leary (eds), *Teaching Excellence in Higher Education: Challenges, Changes and the Teaching Excellence Framework*, 39–74, Bingley: Emerald Publishing.

Wood, P. and M. O'Leary (2019), 'Moving Beyond Teaching Excellence: Developing a Different Narrative for England's Higher Education Sector', *International Journal of Comparative Education and Development*, 21 (2): 112–26.

Yale, A. T. (2019), 'The Personal Tutor–Student Relationship: Student Expectations and Experiences of Personal Tutoring in Higher Education', *Journal of Further and Higher Education*, 43 (4): 533–44.

Yale University Poorvu Center for Teaching and Learning (2020), *Inclusive Teaching Strategies*. Available online: https://poorvucenter.yale.edu/InclusiveTeachingStrategies (accessed 25 January 2021).

Yorke, M. (2004a), 'Employability in the Undergraduate Curriculum: Some Student Perspectives', *European Journal of Education*, 39 (4): 409–27.

Yorke, M. (2004b), *Employability in Higher Education: What It Is – What It Is Not*, Learning and Teaching Support Network (LTSN) series, Learning and Employability, York: Learning and Teaching Support Network (LTSN).

Index

academia 72, 87, 152
academic freedom 55
academic practice 33–4, 36, 55, 57
academics' perspectives 37, 40, 51, 55, 152
accountability 14, 45, 73, 116
Advance HE 29, 80, 89
assessment and feedback 24, 31–2
Australia 19–20, 39, 52
 Australian 19–20, 53

BAME (Black, Asian and Minority Ethnic) 135
barriers 55, 62, 126, 144
BIS (Department for Business, Innovation & Skills) 47, 48
Black Lives Matter 75, 135
blended learning 67, 145–9
Brexit 118, 133
business model 122–3

capital 2, 85–90, 92, 108
career 2, 28, 34, 36, 48, 78, 84–9, 102–3, 109–10, 119, 126, 142, 144, 151–3
CHERI (The Centre for Higher Education Research and Information) 5–6, 42
choices 7, 60, 95, 97–9, 115–16
citizenship 79, 125
civic engagement 13, 116, 119, 121, 126
civic society 80, 115, 128
co-creation 15, 61, 73, 137
co-design 61, 93, 137
collaboration 49, 53, 84, 129, 134, 142
commodification 2, 12, 18, 35, 42–3, 46
commodity 8–9, 13, 17–18, 103
competition 6–8, 12–14, 35, 39, 45, 52, 54, 59, 82, 96–7, 119–20, 122, 136
conceptions 3, 6, 15, 17, 36, 38, 47, 57, 62–3, 73, 75, 87, 103, 108, 134–5, 149

consumerism 3, 5, 8, 10, 103, 114
 consumer 2–3, 7–12, 17, 34, 42, 57–61, 73, 82, 96, 101, 120, 122, 126, 128
COVID-19 pandemic 131, 133, 141–2, 145, 148–9
curriculum 14, 25, 29–30, 58, 77, 79, 82, 84, 87, 89–92, 119, 124, 133–5, 139
customer 3–5, 8–9, 11–12, 14, 17, 42, 47, 57–8, 80, 84, 96, 102, 123, 131
 student-as-customer 11

DfE (Department for Education) 23–4, 27, 29, 31
dialogue 12, 15, 26, 54, 58, 61, 95, 100–2, 105, 111, 113, 118, 123–4, 126, 135, 137, 142, 144, 149
discourses 1, 3, 12, 57, 127, 149

educational technologies 67, 149
education policy 7, 10, 22, 33, 39, 102, 115, 127
employability 3, 33, 49, 61, 77–80, 83–93, 107–10, 119, 125, 133, 152
 graduate employability 77–8, 80, 86–7, 92, 108, 133, 152
employers' perspectives 77–8, 83, 91–2, 152
England 19, 22, 39–40, 57, 60, 73, 95, 98–9, 102, 120–1, 132, 148, 153
EU (European Union) 117–18, 133
excellence
 conceptualization of excellence 16
 idea of excellence 5
 measurement of excellence 6

FE (further education) 12, 39
foundation degrees 85

globalization 122
global ranking 19, 21, 35, 122

governance   24, 116, 124, 128–9
graduate   3, 4, 34, 50, 77–93, 99, 108–10, 119, 126, 133, 152

HEA (Higher Education Academy)   29
HEFCE (The Higher Education Funding Council for England)   22
HEI (higher education institutions)   22, 33, 36, 62, 80, 111, 129, 140

inclusive
　inclusive curricula   133, 138
　inclusive learning and teaching   15, 136
　inclusive pedagogy   15
　inclusive perspective   15, 33, 75, 113, 118, 128–9, 149
indicators   10–12, 44, 52, 103, 107
institutions' perspectives   19, 35
international perspectives   19

JISC (Joint Information Systems Committee)   146–8

knowledge economy   48, 80, 82, 98

leadership   79, 124, 145
league table   19–20, 35, 114, 127
learning and teaching   15, 25, 27–9, 58, 65, 131, 136, 139, 145–8
learning excellence   49, 73

managerialism   12, 54
marketization   35, 46, 52, 57, 59, 73, 76, 79, 96–7, 101, 131
massification   80–1
measurement   2, 4, 6, 10–12, 14, 37–9, 44–6, 50–2, 107–9, 119, 134
mentoring   140, 144
metrics   4, 6, 14, 22, 37, 45–6, 73, 88, 90–3, 97, 102–3, 107–10, 127
MOOC (Massive Open Online Course)   67

neoliberalism   7–8, 13, 16, 122
new public management   5, 14, 16, 21, 52
Northern Ireland   22, 118, 153
NSS (National Student Survey)   9, 11, 22, 25–6, 29, 31, 58–9

OfS (Office for Students)   133, 147
online learning   131–2, 145–8

parents' perspectives   95, 101–2, 111
pedagogy   9–10, 104–5, 136, 138–9
　blended learning pedagogy   145, 148–9
　care and relation-based pedagogy   139–40, 142, 144
　pedagogical approach   15–16, 64
　pedagogic partnership   15, 128, 133
peer learning   26, 49
peer-to-peer learning   48–50, 53, 55
performativity   12, 39, 52, 54–5
Philippines   120, 124–5
plurality   2, 113, 117–18, 128, 134–5
policymakers   34, 39
private benefit   101, 115–16
product   12, 73, 115, 123
productivity   3–4, 12–14, 50–1, 132
proxy   10, 15, 37, 51–2, 81, 83, 110, 127
PT (personal tutor)   32, 140–2, 144
public debate   13, 17–18, 75, 113, 116–17, 119, 123–4, 127–9, 136
public good   1, 11, 13, 15, 50, 80, 89, 115–17, 119–20, 122, 149
purposes of higher education   1–2, 10, 13, 18, 52, 77, 80, 87, 91–2, 100, 103, 115, 119–20, 126–7, 129

QAA (Quality Assurance Agency)   59, 85
quality of teaching   13, 48, 59, 71, 77, 91–2, 119

redbrick university   121–2
REF (Research Excellence Framework)   34–6
rhetoric   3, 8, 41, 45, 51, 111, 115–16, 119
Russell Group   151–2
Russia   19–21, 35

SoTL (scholarship of teaching and learning)   58
staff-student partnerships   60, 137
stakeholder groups   15, 18, 77, 92, 115, 117–20, 136
STEM (Science, Technology, Engineering, Mathematics)   82, 90, 137
student consultant   137–8

student engagement   22, 24–6, 32, 58, 61–2, 68, 74, 136, 142, 151
students as partners   24, 57–60
students' perspectives   57, 62–3, 73–4
student well-being   30, 76, 96, 99–100, 141
SU (the Students' Union)   25, 28, 62

teaching excellence
  measurability and indicators   10–12, 37, 44, 52, 54, 107, 151
teaching quality   15, 19, 20, 22–4, 36, 45, 53, 59–63, 76–7, 95, 97, 100, 110, 119, 124, 151
TEF (The Teaching Excellence and Student Outcomes Framework)   4, 9, 19, 22, 24, 27, 29, 31, 33–5, 37, 45–51, 59–61, 74, 78, 90–1, 96–7, 101, 103, 110, 119, 127, 151
tuition fees   57, 89, 98, 120

UCAS (Universities and Colleges Admissions Service)   48
UK   3–4, 15, 19, 22, 28–9, 35, 37, 39, 42, 47, 51, 53, 59, 62, 74, 78, 80, 83, 90, 96–7, 110, 116–21, 123, 131–3, 140–1, 144, 146–8
UKPSF (The UK Professional Standards Framework)   29
undergraduate   22, 27, 32–3, 47, 59, 62, 65, 74, 77, 85–6, 89–92, 95, 122, 137–8, 141, 148, 153
United States   10, 19, 37, 99, 121, 138
universities
  civic university   119–22, 127
  global university   19–20

value for money   4, 15, 58–9, 103
Vice-Chancellor   28
VLE (virtual learning environment)   146, 148

www.ingramcontent.com/pod-product-compliance
Lightning Source LLC
Chambersburg PA
CBHW061835300426
44115CB00013B/2392